Asterisk

Home Runs, Steroids, and the Rush to Judgment

David Ezra

TRIUMPH
BOOKS

Triumph Books and colophon are registered trademarks of Random House, Inc.

Library of Congress Cataloging-in-Publication Data

Ezra, David, 1963–
   Asterisk : home runs, steriods, and the rush to judgment / David Ezra
      p. cm.
   Includes bibliographical references and index.
   ISBN-13: 978-1-60078-062-2
   ISBN-10: 1-60078-062-8
   1. Bonds, Barry, 1964– 2. Baseball players—Statistics. 3. Doping in sports. I. Title.
   GV865.B637A78 2008
   796.357092—dc22
[B]
                                                        2007034629

This book is available in quantity at special discounts for your group or organization. For further information, contact:

Triumph Books
542 South Dearborn Street
Suite 750
Chicago, Illinois 60605
(312) 939-3330
Fax (312) 663-3557

Printed in U.S.A.
ISBN: 978-1-60078-062-2
Design by Patricia Frey

Contents

Acknowledgments

Many people helped to significantly improve this book. My friend Sal Danna was always there to test an idea or raise a new issue. Ernie Martinez reviewed an early draft of the book and made many helpful suggestions. Countless fine attorneys offered their time, insights, and ideas to help improve the final product, including Kenneth Miller, Michael Grigoli, Jon Miller, Mark Errico, Jim Henshall, Cliff Cohen, and David Hinshaw, just to name a few. Ron Dietch, Stan Bruckheim and my other RFL buddies not only offered important words of encouragement and helpful comments about the book, but they also did so much to maintain my interest in the great sport of baseball. My Berger Kahn co-workers were incredibly supportive. Lisa Stark was kind enough to review parts of the book.

My father taught me all about baseball, and my mother taught me all about hard work. Their influence impacts every page.

Tom Bast and the Triumph Books team had the vision and courage to take on a subject that was a little too controversial for others. I will be forever indebted. They also made the whole process much better than I had a right to expect.

Mark Fainaru-Wada and Lance Williams (*Game of Shadows*), and Jeff Pearlman (*Love Me, Hate Me*) deserve a tremendous amount of credit. Their dedication, hard work, and unusual talents drew my attention to the fascinating issues that surround steroids, baseball, and Barry Bonds, paving the way for a book that looks at the same topic from a different perspective.

Finally, this book owes its life to my wonderful wife Barbara. Not only does she have to live with a guy who *thinks* he's really funny, but then she had to listen to me babble on about baseball and steroids nonstop for two years. Still, from the very beginning she supported the project and the unreasonable demands it placed on my time.

The mistakes are all mine, including the failed attempts at humor. The rest of the book belongs to everyone mentioned above and many unnamed others who contributed their time, energy, and wisdom so generously.

Foreword

I'm sure all the guys in the 500 Club go through the same thing. Over and over again, we hear it: "What do you think about Barry Bonds?" We can't avoid the question. Right or wrong, as he became baseball's most prolific home-run hitter, Barry—a virtual lightning rod for criticism—also become the leading symbol of what many see as baseball's steroid era (roughly 1990–2005). Right or wrong, it seems as if most of the older hard-liners believe he cheated, did something wrong, or beat the system, and they want nothing to do with him. It's the same way they feel about Pete Rose.

The current generation, however, seems a little more tolerant. They're willing to accept his achievements as a product of a commitment to fitness, unique hand-eye coordination, size and strength, longevity, and whatever is or was accepted as normal 10 years ago.

The controversial issue is whether he added size and strength with illegal supplemental help, allowing him not only to do extraordinary things as a hitter but also to extend his years to the point of surpassing the game's most coveted record.

I've gone on record saying if I had played in the 1990s I would have found it hard not to fall to the same temptation, especially when there was no testing and a lax attitude by those in charge. Back then, the game and its players were thriving on the power surge.

Knowing the repercussions as I know them now would have made that decision easy. But being a young player trying to make my mark, be the best I could be, make the most money I could make, and get to the top, I'm not sure I would have said no. More power to those who did. Most people think Barry was not one of them.

Is the assumption that Bonds and others excelled because they juiced justified? Or are today's ultrarich players paying an unfair price for attitudes people perceive as arrogance?

In Barry's case, there's no doubt about one thing—the public sees a surly, "I'm Barry Bonds" attitude and a different set of rules that those around him must accept. There is little about his actions that would, or could, endear him to us.

Hey, who am I to talk? I was a little self-centered in my day as well. A certain amount of it, I'm sure, comes with the territory.

Yet, the perception that today's players have risen to a level of stardom where they have lost touch with the real world seems strong. Television does it. Some of these guys see themselves as rock stars, as entertainers. Maybe they are.

But being full of yourself doesn't mean you cheated. If this book makes you wonder whether some of the hype about steroid-induced home runs is a lot of fiction, it doesn't diminish the accomplishments of the great players who predate the steroid era.

I mean, don't you think most fans believe the home-run king should come from an earlier era, when it was much tougher?

Not my era, mind you. Hank Aaron's era. That's the hard thing to accept, that records set pre-1990 are falling like crazy. I was seventh on the all-time home-run list a little more than 15 years ago; now I'm 12th (with Frank Thomas and Alex Rodriguez chasing fast).

Aaron played his entire career when men were fighting for their livelihood on the field. There were no guaranteed contracts, and pitchers knocked you on your ass if you overswung at an outside pitch. There were no elbow pads to ease the fear of inside pitches. The game policed itself, and only the strong survived.

Today's players are a happy family; many were teammates once. They understand there is a gigantic pie and plenty to go around.

Before free agency started after the 1976 season, players were tied to organizations and forced to be loyal to towns and their fans.

Even through the '80s, many players played for only one organization, which bred a more naturally competitive environment. Today's game is competitive, of course, but not as tough as it was back then. Not so much when I played, but in Aaron's era and before, when you earned your pay year to year. Every year was a free-agent year for them. You don't think hitting was tougher?

I don't blame today's players. They play in the environment they are given. No one forced ownership to pay $20 million a year for a player or to build ministadiums that eventually would destroy the continuity of the record books. Wealthy, egocentric businesspeople and television revenue support this stuff. Don't blame the players, they're just taking advantage of it.

One thing everyone can agree on is this: even if steroids had never been invented, it got easier to hit a home run after 1990. Harder balls, maple bats, small parks, small strike zones, fewer inside pitches, elbow pads, and yes, bigger biceps (whether produced by hours of hard work in a gym or a series of injections in the butt), all combined to increase home-run totals.

If Hank Aaron was a Barry Bonds contemporary, I think he would have hit more than 800 home runs. Maybe a lot more. Hank's reign will never really end. He's the old-school king and will, in my generation, have set the standard in baseball's golden era.

But Barry has had a long, amazingly productive career, a career that most likely will never be matched. He has been a five-tool player most of his career, combining speed, defense, and hitting for average and for power. I lost count of his MVP awards.

I say appreciate it for what it is, the greatest career that spans two highly different generations. I say he is the greatest left-handed hitter of all time, maybe the greatest player (surely of our generation).

Did Barry Bonds use steroids? In my book, *Clearing the Bases*, I answered that question like this: "I don't know." I'm sticking with that same answer for now.

—Mike Schmidt

Introduction

He entered major league baseball as a long and lean lefty. He was swift *and* strong, a talented outfielder with a lively arm. At first, his numbers were more than respectable. But during one off-season he worked out particularly hard. Suddenly, almost out of nowhere, he gained weight and got stronger. The next season he hit more home runs than anyone ever had.

No one could really believe what was happening. A teammate let us in on a little secret: "To understand him you had to understand this: he wasn't human." There must be a better explanation. It probably goes without saying that hard work, God-given talent, and a little bit of good luck are not enough to make a baseball player an all-time record breaker. Certainly, there must be more to it than that. No one could be that good without a special assist—a special something that gives him an edge over everybody else.

To some former players, many devout fans, and more than a few casual observers, the answer is obvious—a player who gains weight, works hard in the off-season, and comes back to have a monster year must really be a monster. That player must be taking so-called performance-enhancing drugs: Deca Durabolin and Winstrol (Stanozolol); tetrahydrogestrinone (THG or the Clear) and Dianabol; human growth hormone (HGH) and Equipoise; the Cream, Insulin, EPO, and Modafinil; or maybe even a little ZMA.

Some assume the worst because of petty jealousy. Some just don't want to believe that their boyhood heroes' records are being broken. Some want to believe drugs equal success because they find a particular player's personality repulsive. Some are just inclined to believe the worst about everyone.

If you make up your mind *before* you carefully examine the evidence, you are going to conclude that the records fell because of steroids. If you *want* to believe records fell because the athlete used steroids, you will try to make the available evidence fit your preconceived conclusions. If you *need* to believe steroids are the reason a particular player excelled, you can avoid close scrutiny of the issue and just believe. This strategy works. At least it works for people who feel comfortable deciding without knowing.

On the other hand, if you want the truth, you can carefully assess the facts behind the attacks—and then you can make up your own mind. Or you can decide not to make up your mind. You might decide that the proverbial jury is still out.

But let's go back to our lanky lefty who suddenly put on all that weight, worked so hard over the off-season, and hit all those home runs. Was he on steroids? If you are one of the many who would love to put the game's greatest player in his place, you already *know* our hard-hitting outfielder was on steroids. After all, it doesn't take a genius to think that a guy who suddenly hits the ball that far that often has to be on the juice.

If you're José Canseco, you believe a player who hits 24 more home runs than he ever hit before must be using steroids, especially if he gained a lot of weight during the off-season. If you're Turk Wendell, the steroid use was "clear just seeing his body."

But the outfielder we have been talking about isn't Barry Bonds—it's George Herman "Babe" Ruth. Early in his career Babe Ruth weighed around 185 pounds. In his last year with the Red Sox (1919), he hit .322 and slugged 29 home runs. But he quickly went from that 185-pound toothpick to a very solid 225 pounds— and that was in his prime, long before he swelled up to the 250-pound behemoth we see in some of the old photos. The new and larger Babe, playing for the Yankees in 1920, hit an unprecedented 54 home runs while batting .376.

Steroids? We know Ruth did a lot of crazy things—but not steroids.

Like so many others, I have been a baseball fan my whole life, but never a Barry Bonds fan. By early 2006, rumors of Bonds's alleged steroid use had been widely circulated. We all heard the rumors, and we probably assumed they were mostly accurate. Why not? The *Sports Illustrated* excerpts of *Game of Shadows* offered a powerful indictment. If solid evidence supported the authors' conclusions, it was going to be hard to deny that Bonds had used steroids and hard to deny that steroids had substantially improved his abilities.

Some of us wanted more than a short article, so we forked over the $26 for Mark Fainaru-Wada and Lance Williams's book. Something seemed to be missing. *Game of Shadows* was supposed to be the definitive compilation of proof that Bonds used steroids. But the authors seemed to start with their conclusions and then work backward to try to make the available "evidence" fit their predetermined conclusions. They ended up with a fascinating book. But it seemed to be one-sided. Was there another side to this story?

Fortunately, it wasn't too late to take a closer look, to look through the "shadows" and into the light, beyond the assumptions that served as support for the accusation that Bonds was a chronic steroid user.

This book's central contention is that the case against Bonds was built on half-truths, speculation, innuendo, assumptions, rationalizations, exaggerations, and flat-out errors. Evidence that tended to exonerate Bonds was too often ignored or minimized. People who criticized Bonds were assumed to be telling the truth.

Information that contradicted the notion that Bonds was a chronic steroid user was discounted.

The problem is far from unique. It happens all the time. When there is a reason to dislike a particular person who is involved in a controversy, it usually takes less evidence to justify an adverse decision. There was, of course, apparent justification for the public's animosity toward Barry Bonds. Mickey Mantle was a mean drunk, but Bonds is a mean sober. What's worse? No matter how badly Bonds might treat other people, no matter how well he plays the role of the modern spoiled professional athlete, it doesn't justify the widespread belief that Bonds hit home runs in bunches because he was a chronic steroid user.

This is not to say that this book's objective is to prove that Bonds didn't try steroids. Let's face it, proving a negative like that is virtually impossible. Instead, the book's objective is more modest—merely to closely scrutinize the available evidence and present the case that the public hasn't really heard about.

Some day, lab tests may show that Bonds had evidence of steroids in his system. If that ever happens, we will have evidence showing that he tried steroids. Even a positive test result, however, will only tell us that he had steroids in his system at a particular point in time. A lab test result will never tell us how often he used steroids. A lab test result will never tell us whether steroids actually turned what would have been ordinary fly balls into home runs.

A positive steroid test result would be a logical place to *start* debating whether Bonds belongs in the Hall of Fame. Ending that debate requires a more complete assessment of all of the available evidence. What if Bonds never does test positive? If he never tests positive, it is even more imperative that we start looking at things from a different perspective. If the case against Bonds has holes in it, Bonds is the greatest living player and he belongs in the Hall of Fame—no questions asked.

The Price of Arrogance

As a personality, Barry Bonds is more like Ann "the Man" Coulter than Stan "the Man" Musial.

Back when Bonds was with the Pittsburgh Pirates, teammate Sid Bream said "everybody in the clubhouse wanted" to kick Bonds's ass "at some point in time." Everyone has had a boss, a coworker, a distant relative, or some other regular acquaintance who can't help but act as if he or she (often a very insecure he) is far superior to everyone else. The world has billions of people, and millions of them like to act as if they are vastly superior to the rest of us. So there is no shortage of Sid Breams—people who want to take a swing at those who feel a need to act as if they are inherently superior.

However, it would be a mistake to see Barry Bonds as just another arrogant professional athlete with a superiority complex. Bonds has taken the image of the ultraspoiled and ridiculously privileged professional athlete and raised it to an entirely different level. And that's why even other arrogant professional athletes can't stand Bonds the man, although they admire Bonds the player.

If his public image remotely resembles reality, Bonds seems to want us to treat him as if he discovered the cure for cancer during his day job, invented a car that runs on tap water while tinkering in the garage on the weekends, and captured and killed Osama bin Laden while he was on a trip to help feed the poor in Afghanistan. He treats people as if he is inherently superior in some meaningful way and as if that point needs to be driven home frequently. Bonds thinks he deserves our respect—not because he has done anything to help

1

the world (or even his community) but because he's really good at baseball. Psychoanalytical types might call it the "Edible Complex"— because if you adopt that attitude, a lot of people are going to want you to eat their fist.

Frank Klopp was a minor league outfielder who briefly played with Bonds for the Pittsburgh Pirates' Prince William minor league affiliate. Bonds needed a place to stay, and Klopp was renting a house that had an extra room. Two weeks after Bonds moved in, Klopp, his wife, and his baby daughter moved out. Klopp explained that Bonds "was never wrong and couldn't accept being wrong. He was a first-round pick, he was Bobby Bonds's son, he was Willie Mays's godson, and he reminded us of that every single day."

Cutting someone down to size didn't satisfy Bonds. He seemed to enjoy sticking the knife in deep and twisting it slowly. When he first started making money as a professional baseball player, his agent was Rod Wright. Ten years earlier Wright was in court working as a public defender when he was approached by someone he didn't know. A man who was charged with drunk driving asked Wright for help. As the man's case was heard, Wright helped coach the defendant with head signals. Following Wright's lead as to proper "yes" and "no" responses, Bobby Bonds, Barry's father, answered the judge's questions, avoided jail, and received probation instead. Bobby tried to pay Wright, but Wright refused, noting that he worked for the county. Bobby, a top major league outfielder, appreciated Wright's integrity, and he hired him as an agent a few weeks later.

Although Wright served as an agent, he was more of a family friend. When Barry Bonds entered professional baseball, it was probably natural for him to hire Wright as his agent. Barry made good money during his first few years, but both Wright and Bonds were looking forward to free agency—a status that would replace Bonds's one-year contract with a long-term deal worth many, many millions of dollars. Needless to say, Wright was shocked when

Bonds fired him before the big-money deal was consummated. The financial blow devastated Wright. The termination hurt Wright's reputation, and it caused him to lose other clients, too. When Wright finally decided he wouldn't be able to change Bonds's mind, he asked for one favor. Could Bonds please talk to Wright's 13-year-old son, Brian, and tell him this was just business? Surprisingly, Bonds agreed to make the call. But Wright says Bonds told his son, "Your dad ripped me off and wasn't doing me right. So I had to do this." Yes, when Bonds set out to hurt someone, he went all the way.

If you believe his detractors, Bonds sees a person's value as a function of his baseball ability. As a result, Bonds's entire world revolves around something most of us see as a moderately pleasurable distraction—baseball. Bonds's take is simple: he is a great baseball player, so we should all worship him.

Let's be fair. Bonds may not be the 100 percent completely despicable human being the media so routinely portrays. There have been isolated reports of instances when he behaved like a normal person and, once in a great while, reports of Bonds acting like a kind and caring person. Don't be fooled—he has the ability to treat people appropriately, if not well. Apparently, however, he chooses to exercise that ability infrequently.

In 2001 Bonds made a very informal bet. If he broke Mark McGwire's home-run record he would buy teammate Shawon Dunston a Mercedes. Dunston had known Bonds a long time, so he wasn't expecting much, even after Bonds hit number 71 on October 5, 2001. Bonds could treat the whole incident as a joke, or maybe Bonds would buy him a very used Mercedes. After hitting two more home runs to reach 73 for the season, Bonds surprised Dunston, presenting him with a brand-new, fully loaded, black Mercedes CL 500.

There were other times Bonds acted like a person people could appreciate. There was the 1987 high school baseball clinic. He got there early despite bad weather, stayed late, and then donated the $500 appearance fee back to the school. There was the time he bought his teammate and workout partner John Cangelosi a new motorcycle for no particular reason. There was the time he wrote a $5,000 check and handed it over to James Mims after Mims explained that he was looking for start-up money for a sporting goods company.

Mergee Donovan thinks Bonds is the greatest. Donovan's son was feeling down after open-heart surgery and she managed to slip Barry Bonds a note, asking if he might find time to try to cheer up her son. Bonds found the time, inviting her son to the next day's game in Milwaukee, and ultimately sending a limousine for the family when the Donovans visited San Francisco. Mergee Donovan describes Bonds as a "wonderful man." Eight years after Bonds's initial act of kindness, the Donovans remain supporters and admirers.

When he played in a summer league, Bonds was assigned to live with a local family, Virg Navarro and her son, Jared. Virg says Bonds taught her son how to cook, brought him to practices, and even called Virg "Mom." Virg says no one believes her, "but Barry was a very loving young man. He became a part of my family." Years later, Bonds helped Jared pay for tuition at Arizona State. According to Virg, Bonds is "pure goodness."

Still, most doubt his sincerity and suspect that his random (and all too rare) acts of kindness were both timed and calculated to help him get that next big contract. As the time to negotiate a contract approached, his agents apparently had to beg Bonds to act like he cared about other people. And everyone seems to agree that his acting skills needed work.

There is one role, however, that Bonds plays better than anyone else. Bonds naturally assumes the role of the arrogant jerk, a guy who treats teammates, fans, reporters—just about everyone—like dirt.

There seems to be a certain something in Bonds that causes him to treat other human beings inappropriately. Perhaps it's his experience as the son of a mildly famous major league outfielder who liked to drink too much. Or maybe the genetic gifts he received in the form of athletic talent came at the price of a genetically instilled social ineptness.

Jim Kaat pitched against Barry's father, Bobby. Kaat says, "Bobby Bonds was a talented player, but he could be belligerent, so I can see where Barry gets that. But Bobby could be charming, too. I haven't seen that side of Barry." In his book on Barry Bonds, Steven Travers tells the story of a man who found himself on a plane, sitting next to the great Willie Mays. The man recognized Mays but did not want to bother him. So he kept quiet. During the flight the man had to ask Mays for a small favor—not an autograph or a ticket request—the kind of little favor one airline passenger asks of another. Travers says Mays supposedly responded with a simple "f*ck you." Mays would become Barry's godfather. Maybe some people who influenced the young Barry Bonds demonstrated contempt for their fellow humans too often.

This book is not going to get to the bottom of exactly why Bonds treats fellow human beings badly. Maybe someday someone will be able to explain *why* Bonds behaved the way he did, but the important point now is that Bonds has managed to cultivate a very negative persona. People who want to get to the truth about Bonds's alleged steroid use need to guard against letting that negativity impact their assessment of the facts.

Bonds supposedly started acting like a jerk long before he became a professional baseball player. Before Kobe Bean Bryant was born, Barry Bonds personified selfishness. When he was in high school,

Bonds asserted himself at a team meeting. Although it was customary for the team to get a small gift for the coach at the end of each season, Bonds asked his teammates, "Why should we get Gort [the coach] anything? What did he do for us?"

When he was in college at Arizona State University, Bonds is said to have broken into a teammate's apartment to steal food from the refrigerator. According to Bonds's angry teammate, "He knew my mom brought this food for me, and here he is, driving a new Trans Am...."

As the son of a relatively wealthy major league baseball player, Bonds never wanted for anything. So his selfishness stood out from the very beginning. And it never subsided. Instead, as Bonds became increasingly wealthy, earning $10 million, $15 million, $18 million, and even $22 million per year, he was just as selfish as he had always been.

In 1997 Bonds wanted the San Francisco Giants' bus to stop at a McDonald's. Although his teammates were accustomed to his selfish ways, some of them were still astonished when Bonds went from player to player, gathering $5 from each of them. Bonds was "only" making a little more than $8.5 million that year.

In 1998 Bonds complained about the quality of the clubhouse food. During a team meeting Bonds announced that each player would contribute $25 each week so the quality of the food could be improved. It didn't bother Bonds that the team included young Latin players who were not making a fortune, players who were sending money to their families back home. Orel Hershiser was nearing the end of his career. He had been an All-Star pitcher with the Dodgers, winning 23 games in 1988. Now he was with the Giants, sharing the clubhouse with Bonds. Hershiser understood that some of his teammates weren't millionaires, so he interrupted Bonds and said, "Barry and I will split the cost so no one else has to." Bonds immediately jumped up and declared, "I ain't paying for nobody!"

Bonds won. Hershiser (who was making about a third of what Bonds was making that year) paid for the food.

When Bonds testified before a federal grand jury in connection with the Bay Area Laboratory Co-Operative (BALCO) investigation, one grand juror asked Bonds whether he had ever considered building a mansion for his trainer, Greg Anderson. Bonds's response was as simple as it was strange: "One, I'm black. And I'm keeping my money." Bonds went on, "There's not too many rich black people in this world. There's more wealthy Asian people and Caucasian and white. And I ain't giving my money up."

But Bonds could be even stranger than that. A company called Famous Fixins created cereals associated with superstar baseball players. In 1999, the company wanted to introduce Barry Bonds MVP Crunch. The personalized line of cereals had worked for Sammy Sosa, Alex Rodriguez, Cal Ripken Jr., and Derek Jeter. And now it was Bonds's turn. Bonds's reaction to a routine request that a percentage of the profits be donated to charity shocked Famous Fixins' cofounder Michael Simon. Although some of the superstars Simon worked with had offered to contribute 100 percent to charity, Bonds responded a bit differently. He became irate. He snapped at Simon, "Why should I hand away my own money?" After all, Bonds said, he had "bills to pay."

Bonds's unusually greedy reaction made an impression on Simon, who says he's "never met anyone like him." As Simon noted, "Here's a guy making millions and millions of dollars, and he would rather have the money go into his pocket." To generate some enthusiasm for the new product, Simon thought it would be helpful for Bonds to sign some memorabilia that could be presented to managers whose stores sold the most Barry Bonds MVP Crunch. When Simon called Bonds to make that suggestion, the reaction was classic Bonds: "Who the f*ck do you think I am?" Then Bonds went on, "Do you think that when Bill Cosby has a book come out the publisher asks him to take the shirt off his back? I don't f*ckin' think so. You have no idea what I've f*ckin' been through. Don't ever f*ckin' ask me...." Simon had had enough; he told Bonds he was a dick and hung up the phone.

Teammates and Staff

Bonds had a way of addressing his teammates that was arrogant, obnoxious, rude, petty, and almost unbelievably self-centered. F.P. Santangelo played in the major leagues for parts of seven seasons. He never hit more than seven home runs in a year. He never hit .300. But he did steal 12 bases for the Giants in 1999. Santangelo received his introduction to Bonds on the second day of spring training. Bonds approached and demanded chewing tobacco from Santangelo. As the story goes, Bonds's approach was direct: "Dude, give it to me. Now!"

Santangelo wasn't going to back down, but he tried to lighten the mood with a little humor. "Bitch," Santangelo teased. "Say please first."

Bonds didn't say please. He responded in traditional Barry Bonds style, shouting, "Do you know who I am?" And then, to more formally introduce himself to his new teammate, he added, "I'm Barry Bonds."

According to Jeff Pearlman, "Barry reveled in picking on the little guy." When Bonds was with the Pirates he managed to bother the team's staff to the point that one team photographer said, "Personally, I hope Barry dies." Bonds was the team's best player. So it must have taken extraordinarily stupid behavior to generate that kind of hatred on the part of a man who was just there to take pictures.

Barry's father, Bobby Bonds, is supposed to have taught his son to throw things around the clubhouse just so the "little guy" employees would be forced to pick up after him. From throwing sunflower seeds at security guards to tossing his used socks around the locker room, Bonds, the son, routinely went out of his way to cause problems for low-paid staff—out of his way to belittle others. According to longtime equipment manager Chuckie Cirelli, Bonds was a "rude, nasty, belligerent person."

Bonds worked incredibly hard to become the best hitter since Ted Williams (maybe the best ever). Unfortunately, it seems as if he worked almost as hard to be unapproachable, obnoxious, and mean.

Mark Ross was a pitcher who ended up with a career record of two wins and two losses. Ross pitched in 27 games for all of 42 innings during his six-year major league career. During one of his two very brief stints with the Pirates, Ross was shocked to find that someone had cut a hole in a shirt he had left in his locker. Ross wondered aloud, whom had he managed to upset? What had he done to unintentionally anger someone? Of course, Ross hadn't done anything to bother any of his teammates. Ross was just too green to know Bonds was born upset. And Bonds was usually willing, if not anxious, to try to belittle or annoy someone. Why would Bonds cut a hole in the shirt of a guy who was struggling just to make the major leagues? No one knows for sure, but it sounds sadistic—like the handiwork of the kind of guy who would throw a little kitten into a clothes dryer and then laugh about the kitten's demise. And, true or not, this is the kind of story people like to tell about Bonds.

Vince Lombardi may have been the greatest football coach in NFL history. He coached the Green Bay Packers to the first two Super Bowl championships while leaving no room for doubt about who was in charge. One former Packers player described Lombardi as very fair, after all, "He treats us all the same—like dogs."

Bonds was no coach. And no one will ever accuse Bonds of being a motivational leader. But there still may be some parallel to Coach Lombardi. Although Bonds may have been particularly comfortable picking on the "little guy," he did tend to treat everyone like dogs, regardless of status. Some might say Bonds was an equal opportunity jerk.

In 1989 Kevin Mitchell hit 47 home runs and drove in 125. He was the National League's Most Valuable Player. In 1990 Mitchell, who was built like a fullback, was having another good year. At the All-Star Game Mitchell ran into Bonds. It was Bonds's first All-Star Game. Bonds greeted Mitchell: "F*ck, Mitch, you shouldn't be starting ahead of me. You're just a fat f*ck."

Mitchell had an interesting background. In his youth, he had been shot several times while he was running with a street gang. He didn't respond directly to Bonds. Instead, Mitchell turned to Bonds's father and calmly whispered, "Get your f*cking son away from me, or I'll beat down his ass and rip out his skull." Since Barry Bonds is still alive, we know Bobby Bonds managed to get him away from Mitchell before Barry could make any more stupid comments.

Willie Stargell played 21 years for the Pittsburgh Pirates, and he retired with 475 home runs (including 48 in 1971). Stargell was a Pittsburgh favorite, and he could expect to be among friends and admirers when he visited Pittsburgh as a coach for the Atlanta Braves. Early in his career, Bonds was in the outfield when he saw Stargell and advised the "old man" to get out. Bonds yelled at Stargell that they had forgotten about him in Pittsburgh. Bonds barked, "I'm what it's all about now."

It took a while for Bonds to realize Stargell didn't think he was funny. When Bonds finally explained that he was "just kidding," Stargell scolded him and advised that he might want to "get some more lines on the back of your baseball card before you talk to me like that."

Kaat was a 25-game winner for the Twins in 1966. After he quit playing he was a Yankees broadcaster for more than a decade. Kaat says Bonds won't even talk to him. According to Kaat, Bonds refuses "even to acknowledge former players."

Dave Parker was the National League's MVP for the Pirates in 1978 (when he hit .334, with 30 home runs, 12 triples, 32 doubles, and 117 RBIs, to go with 20 stolen bases). When Bonds saw Parker at an All-Star Game he couldn't resist asking, "What's an old man like you doing here?" Predictably, Parker wasn't amused. "Listen, ass-wipe," he told Bonds, "I started making All-Star Games when you were in your daddy's stroller."

While it would have been far easier for Bonds to display normal friendliness toward other human beings, he seemed driven to agitate. Whether you were a team photographer or a former MVP, Bonds felt a compelling need to let you know he thought he was a lot better than you were. That's not a great way to make friends.

An odd theme that seems so common to Bonds's interactions with others is a highly inappropriate sense of humor. It was as though Bonds expected people to laugh when he treated them like dirt or when he repeatedly proclaimed his own superiority. If a person was using a drinking fountain, Bonds might use the opportunity to walk up behind him or her, tap the person on the shoulder, and say: "Out of my way. You are not good enough to drink before me." Once in a while that kind of clowning around can be pretty funny. If it is mixed with a healthy dose of self-deprecation, people can find humor in the occasional braggadocio. But with Bonds, the emphasis on his own superiority was constant and unrelenting—and not at all comical.

Bonds had developed his jerk reputation while he was in Pittsburgh. When he went to the San Francisco Giants, he picked up right where he left off. On the very first day of spring training, Bonds walked into the locker room and approached a group of pitchers who were standing around talking. One by one, Bonds stuck a finger in each pitcher's chest and proclaimed, "I own you. I own you. I own you." Did Bonds think he was being funny? Was he expecting to share a laugh with his new teammates? Maybe, but within a few seconds, many of Bonds's new teammates had already decided he came as advertised.

When workouts started, Bonds wore black cleats with orange stripes. He was out of uniform, which required black cleats with white stripes. The team's leader, veteran Matt Williams, told Bonds he should change. Williams had hit almost 90 home runs over the previous three seasons. He would go on to hit 38 homers in 1993 and 43 (in just 445 at-bats) in the strike-shortened 1994 season. Williams was an All-Star in 1990 and a Gold Glove winner in 1991.

So Bonds could have shown a little respect. He could have said something like, "Thanks for reminding me." He could have said that he would get it right tomorrow. Heck, he could have just said, "Sorry about that." Instead, Bonds screamed at Williams in front of the other players, "Dude, I will do whatever I want, whenever I want. Now back out of my face!"

The unidentified Pirate who once said he'd "rather lose without [Bonds] than win with him," probably spoke for many of Bonds's new teammates. No one likes to be around people who have such underdeveloped social skills.

But Bonds was not always such a bad guy. Once, when the Giants were in St. Louis, Bonds spotted a rookie pitcher, Shawn Estes, and took him to lunch. Oddly, however, according to Estes, "The next day I didn't exist."

John Patterson described a similar hot-and-cold routine. Patterson was a reserve infielder who played four years for the Giants. In his major league career, Patterson hit a grand total of five home runs. According to Patterson, "I was a total team player, so I'd talk to anyone about anything." Patterson describes how he'd "be talking to Barry, having a great conversation. Then maybe I'd get up, grab a bat, and come back two seconds later to continue the conversation. He looked at me like I was a piece of shit."

Maybe it was that attitude—treat your own teammates like peons—that led to the bizarre circumstances surrounding Bonds's 500th home run. On April 17, 2001, with a two-ball, no-strike count, Bonds hit a Terry Adams pitch out of Pac Bell Park and into McCovey Cove. More than 40,000 fans made a lot of noise during the historic home run. But when Bonds finished rounding the bases and reached home plate, he was greeted by exactly one teammate—Rich Aurilia, who was already perched on third base when Bonds hit the home run. Aurilia gave Bonds a quick hug and promptly departed. No one else—not one teammate and not one coach—left the dugout to congratulate Bonds.

Bonds had become the 17th major league baseball player to hit 500 home runs in a career. Maybe Bonds remembered what happened when the 16th major league baseball player reached that milestone. When McGwire hit his 500th home run the St. Louis Cardinals players ran from the dugout and charged home plate to swap high fives and congratulate their beloved teammate.

The Media

At the risk of extreme understatement, Bonds doesn't seem to care much about the fact that the media has done so much to help create and perpetuate the societal conditions that allow a person who is adept at hitting a baseball to earn $20 million a year, just for playing a game. He doesn't seem to realize that sports journalists are some of the worker bees who feed a societal mind-set that allows mediocre professional baseball players to make 100 times as much as a great high school teacher. On the other hand, Bonds also doesn't seem to care about the fact that the media could make life particularly challenging for a professional athlete that gets on its bad side. Bonds routinely treated media representatives far worse than other players—even other superstars—treated the media.

When Bonds showed up at the Giants' spring training facility in Scottsdale, Arizona, early in 1993, he was greeted by about 20 reporters. They gathered around Bonds's locker in anticipation of an interview. But Bonds quickly explained that he would not be talking.

The *San Francisco Chronicle*'s C.W. Nevius asked if Bonds would care to make a comment. Bonds replied with a simple, "Nope."

Not so much as "a sentence?" Nevius asked. "A word?"

"No," Bonds sniped. "Do you want to keep pushing?"

When you're treated like that in front of a group of your peers, the sting might linger. And Nevius had a good memory. A couple of years later, Nevius decided that being brutally honest might be a good way to get back at Bonds. He published a column that described Bonds as the "poster boy for everything the angry baseball fan dislikes about the modern player." The article ran under the headline "Trade Bonds and Bring Back the Fans."

A few months later Bonds made a memorable impression on Richard Hoffer of *Sports Illustrated*. Hoffer pointed out that almost everyone who really wanted to interview Bonds ultimately got the chance. But Bonds will always make the writer work extremely hard. With Hoffer, Bonds managed to resist the interview for a full week. At one point he delayed the interview by saying, "Aw, dude! I forgot about stretching!" Since Bonds was the one Giant who almost never stretched with the team, he must have thought that was pretty funny.

But like almost all of the others, after enduring the insults and brush-offs, Hoffer finally got his interview. And Hoffer got the last laugh. Hoffer's article appeared in *Sports Illustrated* on May 24, 1993, and was titled, "The Importance of Being Barry: The Giants' Barry Bonds Is the Best Player in the Game Today—Just Ask Him."

Hoffer's article detailed Bonds's arrogance toward teammates. According to Hoffer, Bonds complained about the fame and fortune baseball bestowed on him by noting: "Well, it's nobody's fault but my own. It's like my dad said, I didn't have to go out there and do all those things, draw this attention to myself. [I] could have been an average player."

Hoffer took the opportunity to remind America about Bonds's repeated playoff failures. He reminded us that the Pittsburgh fans turned on Bonds when the Giants visited Pittsburgh. But the fans' reaction to Bonds was only the tip of the proverbial iceberg. It was actually much worse than that. Bonds went to the Pirates clubhouse expecting a happy reunion. But his former teammates refused to even acknowledge him. And Hoffer made sure we all knew that story, too.

Hoffer explained that maybe it was the time Bonds blamed an injured teammate for a playoff loss. Or maybe it was the time Bonds threw a pizza on R.J. Reynolds during a team flight. Or maybe it was the time in 1991 when Bonds started screaming at some photographers who were trying to take his picture. Since Bonds can do no wrong, he kept yelling at Jim Lachimia, a Pirates public relations specialist. When the melée brought Bill Virdon, a former major league manager and outfielder, to the scene, Bonds shouted at Virdon, "Nobody's going to tell me what to do!" Then, with TV cameras rolling, Bonds directed his anger toward Jim Leyland, the Pirates' manager. According to Hoffer, the argument got so heated Leyland shouted, "I kissed your butt for three years! If you don't want to be here, then get your butt off the field!"

Hoffer says Bonds explained his approach to the media as follows: "I thrive off you guys because I love to make you come back to my locker begging." What a great attitude.

Bonds is the kind of guy who liked to ask reporters if they had gone "to deaf class." So it isn't too surprising that relations between Bonds and the media became so strained that Bonds was rumored to have had "his people" start approaching writers and offering money for articles that said nice things about Bonds.

Occasionally, however, Bonds could show a young writer a good time. In 1994 the Giants were playing the Braves in Atlanta. A young writer who was just two years out of journalism school had been asked to write a short story on the Giants. The journalist was shocked when Bonds motioned across the clubhouse for the scribe to join him. The writer still couldn't believe a one-on-one interview with Barry Bonds was about to ensue. So the writer asked, "Me?"

"Yeah, you," Bonds responded. Then Bonds produced the most recent copy of *Playboy* magazine and asked the young writer, "Have you ever seen anything like this?" Bonds thumbed through the magazine, showing the young writer each heavily airbrushed photograph, page by page, photo by photo.

So this was proof—Bonds could share some "good fun" with a sportswriter. Unfortunately, there was one small problem—the young journalist was a woman, a woman who saw Bonds's behavior as offensive and unprofessional. Noting that she had never previously interacted with Bonds, the young female writer politely suggested that "something was off with him."

The same hot-and-cold treatment that had bothered Patterson and Shawn Estes could also be used with the media. When Bonds was with the Pirates, a member of the Pittsburgh sports press was invited to golf with Bonds. Chasing the little white ball for 18 holes gives you time to get to know someone. But when the writer saw Bonds the next day—less than 24 hours after the golf outing—Bonds refused to even acknowledge the writer. Not so much as a simple, "Hi."

Bonds had other strategies for disrespecting writers, too. It was a special talent—he could be obnoxious in many different ways. Or maybe it's fun to refuse to look at the person who is trying to interview you. Maybe it's fun to respond to every question during an interview with, "Whatever, dude." Maybe it's fun to turn on a tape recorder during interviews and subtly threaten to sue reporters who are just trying to earn a living.

The Fans

Bonds could see no point in treating writers like human beings. But what about the fans? What about the people who actually pay money to watch baseball—money that ends up in the players' bank accounts?

Well, Bonds doesn't need to show the fans any respect either. He doesn't see that as part of his job description. Bonds rationalizes his mistreatment of fans this way: if a fan pays $10 to see a movie starring Jack Nicholson, the fan doesn't "expect to get Jack Nicholson's autograph." There may be a weaker rationalization, but I can't think of it.

During the 2003 All-Star break, Bonds was discussing his chances of eclipsing Hank Aaron's career home-run record (755). Bonds explained, "The only number I'll care about is Babe Ruth's. That's it—715. Because [that would mean] as a left-handed hitter, I wiped him out. That's it. And to the baseball world, Babe Ruth is Baseball, am I right? I got his slugging percentage and I'll take his home runs, and that's it. Don't talk about him no more."

Most major league baseball players understand that without Babe Ruth, they might be working at Wal-Mart. As Waite Hoyt, the great Yankees pitcher who was inducted into the Hall of Fame in 1969, once said, "Every big leaguer and his wife should teach their children to pray, 'God bless Mommy, God bless Daddy, and God bless Babe Ruth.'"

But Bonds—the man teammates had nicknamed "I-I-Me-Me"—wouldn't even show respect to Babe Ruth; so why show it to the fans?

The great Rogers Hornsby once explained that "any ballplayer that don't sign autographs for little kids ain't an American. He's a communist." Well, at least for some, times have changed. When Bonds was with the Giants, a reporter saw Bonds walk by two kids who were leaning over the railing and begging for his autograph. According to the reporter, Bonds looked up at the two children and said, "You little shits, leave me the f*ck alone!"

In the middle of his third major league season (June 1988) the Pirates were about to play the Mets at Three Rivers Stadium when Bonds unloaded on a group of young autograph seekers, telling them to "F*ck off! F*ck off! F*ck off! F*ck off!" This same kind of thing happened often enough to motivate R.J. Reynolds to upbraid Bonds in public. Reynolds spent eight seasons in the major leagues. In 1989 he hit .270 and stole 22 bases for the Pirates. After yet another episode of Bonds's mistreating people, Reynolds scolded Bonds: "Be a f*cking man, Barry. Treat people with dignity!" Bonds needed that kind of scolding a lot more often than he actually received it.

Bonds has never liked to give his autograph. Even when the Giants' owner, Peter Magowan, wanted Bonds to sign a few baseballs, Bonds refused. Bonds's reluctance to sign was pronounced to the point that Charlie Hayes could tease him about it. Hayes was a veteran major leaguer who once hit 25 home runs in a season. As his career was winding down, he spent two seasons with the Giants. When Bonds refused to sign a ball for him, Hayes told Bonds he already had Sammy Sosa's autograph, and "it's worth a hell of a lot more than yours!"

Ron Kittle played 10 years in the major leagues; one year with the White Sox he hit 35 home runs and drove in 100 runs. Kittle says he once approached Bonds in the visitors' clubhouse at Wrigley Field and asked him to sign some memorabilia for a charitable cause. Kittle was raising money for cancer, and he had purchased a game-worn Bonds jersey that he hoped Bonds would sign. According to Kittle, Bonds not only declined, but he did it with flair, proclaiming that "I don't sign for white people."

Kittle, who stands 6'4" and weighs 220 pounds, says he's only been really angry a few times in his life. This was one of those times. He was ready to "kick his ass," but Matt Williams, who overheard the incident, intervened. Williams told Kittle, "That's just the way he is." Still, Kittle told Bonds, "White people aren't the only ones who get cancer." Kittle says, "Bonds just turned his back on me and walked out of the clubhouse."

Bonds denies Kittle's account, sort of. Kittle's recollection prompted Bonds to ask, "Who is Kittle? How long did he play? He played in our league?" But the statement Kittle says he heard does sound like vintage Bonds. This is, after all, the same person who noticed something was missing from his locker and allegedly thought it was really funny to scream out, "I don't want any white bastards in my locker!"

On the other hand, there *is* something wrong with Kittle's story. In *Ron Kittle's Tales from the White Sox Dugout*, a book Kittle published in 2005, Kittle says it was 1992 when he purchased the Bonds jerseys "with San Francisco on the front and his name and No. 25 on the back." Of course, in 1992 Bonds played for the Pirates, and he wore No. 24. But maybe Kittle's book just had the year wrong.

The Jerk

Not all of Bonds's negativity is directed at baseball-related matters. Bonds is filled with negative energy. According to his first wife, Sun, Bonds regularly beat her. He got angry after she told him she was taking a job he did not want her to accept and allegedly kicked her in the back and ribs even though she was eight months pregnant. During another argument, he allegedly hit her with a closed fist, causing her to fall into a bathtub while she was holding their baby boy. That may be exaggerated or maybe even fabricated, but it is the kind of accusation that helps shape the public's opinion.

Bonds has always had an uncanny ability to agitate. In 1987 Bonds hit 25 home runs and stole 32 bases for the Pittsburgh Pirates. His teammate, Brian Fisher, pitched well enough to win 11 games and throw three shutouts. Fast-forward 10 years. It's 1997, and the Giants are playing the Rockies in Colorado. A Rockies clubhouse attendant approached Bonds and explained that he was a friend of Fisher's.

The clubhouse attendant reminded Bonds that Fisher had pitched for the Pirates and was once Bonds's teammate.

Bonds was already visibly annoyed with this inappropriate use of his time. But he held back, giving the clubhouse attendant time to make his point—Fisher's son had been diagnosed with cystic fibrosis (and died the following year). Fisher holds an annual fund-raiser to fight cystic fibrosis. The clubhouse attendant explained, "Brian was wondering if you would sign a couple posters and balls that they could raffle off." The attendant was telling Bonds that other players, such as Larry Walker and Randy Johnson, had contributed, when Bonds decided he had had enough and cut him off. Bonds didn't just refuse to sign. He did not politely decline. He did not say he was too busy or too tired. Instead, Bonds told the clubhouse attendant, "F*ck you," then ended the conversation by adding, "And f*ck Brian Fisher."

So, although Kittle probably got the date wrong, his story is not the only time we have heard about Bonds viciously attacking when he was asked to donate a little of his time to help others.

At the beginning of the 2002 season, Joseph Lang and Paul Scott, two groundskeepers at Pittsburgh's PNC Park, were killed in a motor vehicle collision. They were driving to the stadium when a sport utility vehicle broadsided their car. Both died, and neither had life insurance. Photographer Dave Arrigo helped to organize a photo auction with proceeds to go to the deceased groundskeepers' families. When teams would come to Pittsburgh, Arrigo would describe the tragedy and note that one of them had three little girls and the other had a son. Arrigo would ask the opposing team's star players to sign photographs that could be auctioned off to help the families. Sosa sent a bat and four pictures. Jeff Bagwell, Craig Biggio, Randy Johnson, and Curt Schilling were "more than willing to help." When the Giants came to town Arrigo approached Bonds. After all, Arrigo remembered Bonds from the days when Bonds was with the Pirates.

Bonds's approach to the tragedy was simple. He told Arrigo, "I ain't signing shit." Then he walked away.

What a guy. Do you *want* to believe his success is a direct result of rampant steroid use? Of course you do!

Bonds's default setting is nasty and obnoxious. Rick Reilly, the entertaining *Sports Illustrated* columnist, was working on an article involving police who pull over motorists based on skin color. Reilly approached Bonds and inquired: "Barry, I was just wondering if you've ever been pulled over for DWB."

A flummoxed Bonds didn't know what DWB meant. Instead of asking Reilly to explain the reference ("driving while black"), Bonds screamed at Reilly, "Get the f*ck out of my face!" A now irate Bonds continued, "What the f*ck? What kind of f*cking question is that?" Bonds was a little less steamed after a teammate politely explained the reference. That's the kind of person Barry Bonds has been: assume the worst about everyone, attack if you don't know what else to do.

The way he mistreats people suggests that Bonds must really be miserable inside. But some people are just a bit sadistic, able to enjoy the suffering of others. So who knows? For our purposes, the reasons Bonds acts out aren't that important.

A columnist for the *San Jose Mercury News*, Ann Killion, puts it this way: "Barry is one of those guys who has everything—all the talent in the world, all the money in the world. But I think he has kind of a shitty life." She's probably right.

When Mike Schmidt published his book, he offered a little advice for Bonds. Schmidt volunteered:

> Barry Bonds is a friend. I have played against him, done public appearances with him, interviewed him, hit my 500th home run over him, and admired him for his recent accomplishments. My suggestion to Barry, and this comes from personal experience, would be to make the needs of people

around him more important than his own. That would create some good karma, something Barry—like the rest of
us—needs. It might even make people want him to break
Hank Aaron's HR record.

Bonds would do well to heed Schmidt's advice. If Bonds were to
demonstrate concern for his fellow human beings that came anywhere
close to approaching the concern he always shows for himself, it
would help Bonds in the public relations department, help him in
dealing with the press, and help maximize the likelihood that he will
be remembered as baseball's greatest player, not merely regarded as
its most prominent cheater. He needs to start giving—giving his time
and his money. Immediately starting to treat others with respect and
dignity would maximize Bonds's chances of prevailing in the legal
squabbles he is anticipating. It would also help maximize his chance
of promptly entering the Hall of Fame when he becomes eligible.

Most important, by demonstrating empathy and showing respect
toward others, Bonds would probably start feeling better about
himself. He might even start to enjoy life. Either that or Bonds can
continue to treat other people like dogs. And if he lives long enough,
he might someday be downgraded from "extreme narcissistic maniac"
to "cantankerous old man" —kind of like Ted Williams.

Any decent attorney knows one way to increase the chances of getting
a good result for a client is to enable the decision maker (whether judge,
jury, or arbiter) to sympathize with the client. If the attorney can't do
that, maybe there is a way to demonize the other side, revealing its
greed, bad motives, or inappropriate conduct. Sometimes all it takes
are a few carefully chosen words that highlight the negatives. The
better attorneys can do this in a subtle way so that they don't appear

to be attacking the opposition. A decision maker that doesn't like a particular side will tend to view the facts and law more favorably toward the party that is perceived as good or even neutral. The bad guy is fighting an uphill battle because the decision maker doubts what that person says and can't help but think that justice requires an adverse ruling or verdict.

In a way, Bonds is facing the worst of both worlds. On one side of the fight stand Babe Ruth and Hank Aaron. Whatever their flaws, they are revered if not worshiped. Each baseball fan who thinks about Bonds and steroids comes to the decision-making process knowing that unless Bonds was on steroids, he is going to be regarded as the undisputed home-run king. Hank Aaron's all-time home-run record will belong to Bonds. They know that unless Bonds was on steroids, he could be considered the greatest player who ever played baseball, surpassing Babe Ruth.

To this extent, Bonds stands in the shoes of Roger Maris (who chased and surpassed Babe Ruth's single-season home-run record) and, ironically enough, Hank Aaron (who chased and surpassed Babe Ruth's career home-run record). Both Maris and Aaron faced adversity and animosity as they chased down the Babe. But Bonds faces a challenge Maris and Aaron never faced. Because of the way he has treated so many people, Bonds has managed to demonize himself. Even casual baseball fans often see Bonds as a very bad person who does not deserve to be breaking records held by the all-time greats. They feel sorry for Babe Ruth and Hank Aaron, both of whom are generally regarded as deserving heroes. And because they don't like him, it is easy to believe justice would be served if Bonds is adjudged a steroid addict who deserves an asterisk next to his name in the record books—a steroid addict who does not belong in the Hall of Fame.

Is this the karma Schmidt wrote about? Bonds's abysmal personality has created a situation in which an apparent majority of those who follow baseball want bad things to happen to him. According to one ESPN poll, as he approached number 756, 52 percent of fans were hoping Bonds would fail in his quest to break Aaron's all-time home run record. They want to believe Bonds was a steroid user who broke the single-season home-run record because he used steroids. They want to believe Bonds was able to chase Aaron's all-time home-run record only because he used steroids.

In May 2006, just months before the tragic plane crash that killed him, pitcher Cory Lidle shared his thoughts about Bonds and the home-run chase:

> It's sad. I'm not a player-hater. I like to see players get paid as much as they can. But without friggin' cheating. What he could have done without performance-enhancing drugs—which he hasn't been proven guilty of, which I'm not buying—you can maybe take what he had done in his prime, before his head started growing at an enormous rate, and just make those projections. Say that, "This is what he could have done." Maybe it's 550 home runs. I don't know. It definitely wouldn't have been anything close to 700. I don't want to see him break records. If he breaks them, it will be a shame because I think when all is said and done, the truth will come out. It hasn't yet, but I think if he was in front of a jury, and there had to be a verdict...I think the verdict might be guilty.

Being a notoriously bad person doesn't mean you are a steroid addict. However, being a notoriously bad person does mean it will be harder to convince people that all those home runs were the product of hours spent in the weight room, as opposed to regularly bending over so Greg Anderson could inject your rear end full of steroids. Too many people want to give Anderson and steroids credit for what

Bonds accomplished. But it is possible to hate Bonds the person while respecting Bonds the baseball talent. And it is possible to evaluate the evidence of Bonds's alleged steroid use in a more neutral and evenhanded way. If you do that, you'll probably find that the case against Bonds has more than a few holes.

The sad fact is, however, that up until now only one side of this story has been told. We've been bombarded with articles, books, and commentary that attack Bonds the person and pound on his alleged steroid use as if it had been proven. No one who wants to address the possibility that Bonds was not a chronic steroid user has been given a fair hearing. Have we sold fans short—perhaps incorrectly assuming that their dislike for Bonds is so great that they are not interested in the evidence that tends to exonerate Bonds?

2

Talent and Hard Work

The Barry Bonds we usually hear about is a horrible human being. And that makes it easy for many to want to believe Bonds used steroids—the juice that led to all the home runs. Whether the stigma is well deserved or not, we know a lot of people want Bonds to fail; they want Bonds to be permanently branded with a steroid asterisk. There's no shortage of people who want to see Bonds imprisoned for perjury or tax evasion. But even those who can't stand Bonds the person reluctantly have to acknowledge his incredible talents and unmatched dedication as a baseball player.

Curt Leskanic was a hard-throwing right-hander who pitched in the major leagues for 11 seasons. He was in his third season with the Colorado Rockies in 1995. During his first two seasons in the majors, the Rockies often used him as a starting pitcher. But by 1995 the Rockies had stopped using Leskanic as a starter, and that was probably the best year of Leskanic's career. He saved 10 games while allowing only 83 hits in 98 innings, and he struck out 107 batters while walking only 33.

Near the end of the 1995 season, the Rockies were playing the Giants at Candlestick Park. Leskanic seemed to be particularly tough that day. After John Patterson struck out, he came back to the Giants' dugout and wondered out loud, "How does anyone hit this guy?"

Bonds had never been one to give away his secrets, but he must have felt bad for Patterson. Or maybe he just felt like showing off a little. Bonds blurted out, "When Leskanic turns his glove he's throwing a slider, and when he comes in straight it's a fastball."

Patterson, and some of his more talented teammates, such as Matt Williams, closely scrutinized Leskanic's delivery. So did the team's manager, Dusty Baker (who had hit 242 home runs during his 19 major league seasons as a player, primarily with the Braves and Dodgers). No one could see anything about Leskanic's delivery that would tip his pitches. Baker accused Bonds of making it up: "You're shitting us—there's nothing there."

So Bonds started predicting Leskanic's pitches. Bonds called a fastball, and Leskanic threw a fastball. Bonds called another fastball, and Leskanic threw another fastball. Bonds predicted a slider. Here comes a slider. Bonds went back to the fastball, and Leskanic threw a fastball.

The episode left Bonds's teammates and manager a little stunned. Bonds had correctly called every pitch Leskanic threw. He had seen something in Leskanic's delivery no one else could see—not even after Bonds had clued them in.

Bonds saved such performances for special occasions, usually hoping for the maximum "shock-and-awe" factor. He was able to repeat the pitch-calling routine during an All-Star Game, where he called out the type of pitch the American League pitcher was throwing as the ball was leaving the pitcher's hand. The best players in the National League sat on the bench expressing disbelief and amazement. Steroids and HGH don't help you study pitchers to the point where you can call their pitches in advance.

Brainpower, or at least intelligence for the game, is an attribute that sets Bonds apart from other players. He has studied pitchers closely. And, although it was unusual for a position player, Bonds often attended pitchers' meetings. He wanted to know how pitchers thought. He wanted to know what to expect, what pitch was likely to be coming next. Attendance at the meetings also helped him play left field. By knowing what his own team's pitcher was thinking, he could better gauge likely outcomes and better position himself in the outfield.

Pitcher Jeff Juden played eight years in the major leagues. He split the 1996 season between the Giants and the Montreal Expos. During a spring training intrasquad game he had an encounter with Bonds that made an impression. Juden was standing near Bonds as Bonds was starting the on-deck ritual. Bonds made a little prediction for Juden: "This guy's going to start me with a...fastball inside to try to back me off the plate. Then he's gonna throw the change-up down and away. I'm going to sit on both those pitches, and then he's going to try and sneak a fastball by me. I'll take him out on that pitch to left field."

"Yeah, right," thought Juden.

Pitcher Steve Mintz delivered the first pitch, an inside fastball. The second pitch, an outside change-up. Next came the fastball Bonds was waiting for. Bonds hit the ball hard to left field, a long home run. The episode left Juden bewildered. It was "one of the most amazing things" Juden had ever seen. But Bonds "didn't say how he knew what was coming."

In *Game of Shadows*, Mark Fainaru-Wada and Lance Williams boldly conclude that steroids allowed Bonds to keep playing at "what should have been the end of his baseball career." When they were writing their powerful summary of the case against Bonds, Fainaru-Wada and Williams had no way of knowing that Bonds would some day rewrite the elderly section of the baseball record book. As he turned 43 during the 2007 season, Bonds was now subject to steroid testing and closely scrutinized for any hint of impropriety. Bonds hit 28 home runs in just 340 at-bats. His 8.2 home run percentage was better than his 1992 season (7.1 percent)—a season Bonds started at age 27. In the long history of baseball, no player who started a season at age 42 had ever hit as many as 20 home runs. Carlton Fisk—another player who started working out late in his career—previously held the record with 18 in 1990.

The *Shadows* authors acknowledge that Bonds was "an outstanding player and a likely Hall of Famer" before steroids allegedly boosted his abilities. But they still seem to discount the intelligence, dedication, and genetic gifts Bonds brought to the game. In 2006 and 2007, at an advanced age in baseball terms, while facing the pressure of the home run record pursuit, without Greg Anderson, while subject to steroid testing, with a possible perjury indictment hanging over his head, and while being scrutinized (not to mention, criticized) to an extent most of us can't even imagine, Bonds led the major leagues in on-base percentage—both years. In 2007, no one even approached Bonds. Not Alex Rodriguez (31), Albert Pujols (27), or Vladimir Guerrero (31).

Some contend that genetics are the single most important attribute of great athletes. And to a certain extent, it's true. In basketball, you can't teach height, as they say. And a baseball player's hand-eye coordination, arm strength, and speed are essential tools that seem to be something a person is born with or without.

What do genes tell us about a player's ability? Well, some might argue that knowing the family tree tells us absolutely nothing about a player's capabilities. But there are many examples of baseball skill that runs in the family. Dizzy Dean and his brother, Paul "Daffy" Dean, pitched for the famous 1934 St. Louis Cardinals, known as the Gashouse Gang, that beat the Detroit Tigers in a hard-fought World Series. Both Deans had worked on the family farm picking cotton. After an injury disabled their father, Paul Dean took a job pumping gas, and Dizzy joined the army so that he could make $21 per month. Dizzy probably went no further than third grade in school, but he was blessed with a great arm. And despite his humble beginnings, he was full of confidence. When Paul joined Dizzy with the Cardinals, Dizzy predicted they would combine to win 45 games. They did better than that—Paul won 19 and Dizzy won 30. In the World Series, Paul won two games, and Dizzy won two games.

In September, with the Cardinals fighting for the pennant, Dizzy opened the first game of a doubleheader against the Dodgers by pitching a three-hit shutout. Paul followed in the nightcap by pitching a no-hitter.

"I wished I'd have known Paul was going to pitch a no-hitter," Dizzy observed. "I'd have pitched one, too." The Deans were good.

The Dean brothers comprise only one of many great baseball families: Tommie and Hank Aaron; Joe, Dom, and Vince DiMaggio. The Boone family, comprised of Ray, Bob, Bret, and Aaron, was a three-generation baseball family. There were the Alou brothers. Ken Griffey Sr. and Ken Griffey Jr. The Alomars—Sandy Sr., Sandy Jr., and Roberto. Yogi Berra and his son, Dale. George and Ken Brett. José and Ozzie Canseco—well, maybe that's not a great example. Despite all the steroids, poor Ozzie never did manage to hit a home run in the major leagues (meanwhile, José hit 462 dingers).

To the extent genetics are a factor in a baseball player's success, Barry Bonds was born to succeed. His father, Bobby Bonds, played 14 years in the major leagues. Bobby played for the Giants for seven years, starting in 1968. He also played with the Yankees, the Angels, and several other teams before he called it a career in 1981 at the age of 35.

Bobby was very talented. He typically hit leadoff because of his speed. But he was unusually powerful for a leadoff hitter. He revolutionized the leadoff spot. Never again would it be confined to soft-hitting middle infielders who tried to slap singles to the opposite field. In 1973 Bobby hit 39 home runs. He also stole 43 bases. Bobby made 30-30 a habit, regularly hitting 30 or more home runs and stealing 30 or more bases in the same season. He hit as high as .302 in 1970, when he collected 200 hits. In 1977, playing for the Angels, Bobby managed to drive in 115 runs and still steal 41 bases. He finished his career with 332 home runs and 461 steals. Bobby was a three-time All-Star and a three-time Gold Glove winner.

Bobby was something of an athletic prodigy. According to a boyhood friend, Bobby's high school was facing an archrival in both baseball and track, simultaneously. When the 100-yard dash was set to start they called a timeout in the baseball game. Bobby jumped the center-field fence to get to the starting line, and he ran the 100-yard dash in 9.8 seconds—while dressed in his baseball uniform and wearing cleats. He returned to the baseball diamond and played a few more innings before it was time for the long jump. As his friend Dickie Jackson recalled, Bobby "returns to the track and broad jumps 24 feet, 11 inches. That was in baseball cleats, too. I swear to God that happened. He was that good."

Barry and Bobby did not have the greatest father-son relationship. Apparently, Bobby became an alcoholic during his playing days, and the travel he had to endure as a professional baseball player limited the time he could spend with Barry and his other children.

Bobby wasn't really known for being the most intelligent player on the field. Even after his career ended and Bobby joined the Giants as a hitting coach, most of the players he coached were not impressed. Nevertheless, Barry has credited his father for giving him the mental edge that made him the greatest hitter of all time. Discussing the subject of cheating, Barry shared this insight: "I'll tell you how I cheat. I cheat because I'm my daddy's son. He taught me the game. He taught me things nobody else knows. So that's how I cheat. I'm my daddy's son."

Bobby's brother was good enough to be drafted by a professional football team. His sister once held the women's record in 80-meter hurdles. She was on the 1964 U.S. Olympic team. Maybe there was something in those genes.

From the moment he was born, Barry Bonds was surrounded by baseball greatness. Dusty Baker was a close friend of the Bonds family—so close, it is said, that he actually changed Barry's diapers on occasion. "Mr. October," Reggie Jackson, who hit 563 regular-season home runs plus 18 in the postseason and five in the 1977 World Series, is Bonds's distant cousin. The great Willie Mays is a

Hall of Famer who hit 660 home runs and stole 338 bases, mostly while playing center field for the Giants. Mays was a two-time National League MVP and a perennial Gold Glove winner. With the Giants, Mays was Bobby's teammate, and he was destined to become Barry's godfather. Barry the toddler took naturally to Mays, the baseball god of his day.

No one can remember a time when Barry struggled athletically. As a teenager Bonds was not known as a particularly hard worker. In fact, he leaned in the opposite direction. But things changed. As the competition got better, Bonds's desire to be the best manifested in a work ethic few could match. Charlie Hayes remembers a day when he had to retrieve something from the stadium. He may not remember what he had to get, but he remembers arriving at 7:00 in the morning, "And there was Barry, doing yoga for the past one and a half hours. While most of us were getting out of bed, Barry was up pumping iron and running. He was aware that being great meant busting your ass."

By the mid-1990s Bonds had started off-season training with the San Francisco 49ers' legendary wide receiver Jerry Rice. Rice was known as the most dedicated and hardest-working football player in the NFL. In the mornings the duo ran a five-mile trail that included an expansive uphill section. At night they focused on weight training, alternating between upper body and lower body. They did 21 different exercises, three sets of 10 repetitions each. At the time, Jim Warren was Bonds's personal trainer. Warren couldn't believe the dedication Bonds displayed. He explained:

> I've trained a couple hundred NFL players and probably 50 Major League Baseball players and a ton of world-class sprinters and triathletes, but in 25 years I've never found anyone who took training as seriously, with as much passion and commitment, as Barry. I've never had anyone

show up early, work hard, stay on task, do the shit nobody
wants to do, and stick with it every single day.

Bonds also possessed an unparalleled determination. When Bonds
started with the Pirates he had speed and power, but defensively, he
was merely respectable as an outfielder. In 1988 Bonds's teammate,
Andy Van Slyke, won a Gold Glove. The trophy was shipped to the
clubhouse and, according to Van Slyke, it "was a very cool-looking
piece of hardware." Bonds spent significant time admiring Van Slyke's
trophy. Finally, he promised that "next year, I'm going to win me one
of these." Bonds did not win the Gold Glove in 1989. But he did win
one in 1990. And in 1991. And in 1992. And every year through 1998
with the exception of 1995. Van Slyke and Bonds were never great
friends. In fact, they seemed to hate each other. Bonds sometimes
referred to Van Slyke as "the great white hope." But even Van Slyke
had to acknowledge that when Bonds "decides to get something
done, he gets it done."

Bob Pettit scored more than 20,000 points and grabbed more than
12,000 rebounds during his NBA career. He was Rookie of the Year,
a two-time Most Valuable Player, and an All-Star 11 times. Pettit was
known as a fierce competitor with an unparalleled work ethic. After
Pettit had been cut from his high school basketball team, he spent
hours shooting at a basketball hoop that had been reduced to 14-
inch diameter, instead of the usual 18 inches. When Pettit played in a
regulation game, the basket looked pretty big.

Bonds was never cut from a team (although his difficult personality
caused his college teammates to temporarily vote him off the team).
Unlike Pettit, Bonds displayed extreme talent from the earliest age.
Like Pettit, however, Bonds developed a work ethic that set him apart
from his contemporaries.

Bonds has also borrowed from Pettit's approach to practice, often using equipment and techniques that increase the level of difficulty. During the mid-1990s he started practicing by hitting against a pitching machine that was throwing baseballs that were smaller—and therefore harder to hit—than regulation size baseballs. Occasionally, Bonds would use a smaller bat as well, to increase the level of difficulty even more. He sometimes takes batting practice with his right eye closed, a technique that is believed to improve the left eye, enabling Bonds to wait just a little longer on a pitch.

To sharpen his concentration and batting eye, Bonds writes numbers on tennis balls. When the tennis balls are pitched to him, he tries to read the number—while the ball is in midflight. His goal is to swing only at odd-numbered balls. Think about that for a second. Although it may sound impossible to accomplish, this exercise develops discipline, concentration, and focus.

*

To become the greatest hitter ever, it takes more than good genetics, hard work, and a challenging practice routine. There has to be an incredible talent to build from. When he was at Arizona State, Bonds is said to have "played his ass off" when scouts were watching. And he could be something of a showoff, displaying the raw talent that would ultimately translate into hitting accomplishments so phenomenal that only Babe Ruth could serve as a measuring stick.

In 1985, when Arizona State held its annual alumni game, a small group of major league players were watching the team take batting practice against a pitching machine. The machine was delivering baseballs at 85 mph when Barry stepped in and started hitting line drives. It's hard to show off against a machine that is "only" throwing 85 mph. So, between each pitch, Bonds took a step toward the pitching machine. He continued hitting, and he continued stepping forward, moving closer and closer so that his permissible reaction time was less and less. Bonds continued to hit 85 mph pitches while he was standing just 30 feet from the machine, rather than the usual 60 feet, six inches. According to one of the many observers, "None of the big leaguers even thought about trying it. Barry was superhuman."

Like the great Ted Williams, Bonds was also blessed with extraordinarily keen eyesight. This example may be a slight exaggeration, but people have said Bonds is able to read the words on freeway exit signs when other people in the car are just starting to recognize that there is a sign up the road. When Bonds's subsequent accomplishments are examined and treated as evidence or proof of steroid use, it is important to keep his basic talent base in mind. Obviously, 73 home runs is an enormous single-season quantity. But it isn't proof of steroid use—at least not in Bonds's case.

If the St. Louis Cardinals' shortstop, David Eckstein, hit 70 home runs in a single season it would make sense to look for an explanation that went well beyond Eckstein's God-given talent and his incredible commitment. At 5'6" and 170 pounds, Eckstein makes the most of his abilities. He was the World Series MVP in 2006 and the starting shortstop for two different world championship teams over a five-year span. In some ways, Eckstein is the most inspiring player in the game, standing as living proof that extreme desire coupled with a little luck and a lot of hard work can lead almost anyone to the highest levels of professional sports. Eckstein probably had his best year in 2002. He hit .293, slamming eight home runs (a career high) while stealing 21 bases for the world champion (now comically named) Los Angeles Angels of Anaheim.

If Eckstein suddenly gained 20 pounds and hit 50 home runs, we would have to consider crediting steroids for the sudden display of power. So far, Eckstein's career offers no hint of a possible hot streak that would allow the shortstop to hit 50, or even 35, or even 20 home runs in a season.

To put it mildly, Barry Bonds is not David Eckstein. Even those who have attacked Bonds the most relentlessly don't accuse him of using steroids until after the 1998 season ended. How good was Bonds before 1999? He started his major league career with the Pittsburgh Pirates in 1986. In his first four major league seasons he was used primarily as a leadoff hitter, and he was still learning the game. Remove those first four seasons (in which his goal was usually to get on base and steal bases), and his statistics through 1998 look like this:

Yr.	G	AB	R	H	HR	RBI	SB	BB	SO	BA	OB	SG
1990	151	519	104	156	33	114	52	93	83	.301	.406	.565
1991	153	510	95	149	25	116	43	107	73	.292	.410	.514
1992	140	473	109	147	34	103	39	127	69	.311	.456	.624
1993	159	539	129	181	46	123	29	126	79	.336	.458	.677
1994	112	391	89	122	37	81	29	74	43	.312	.426	.647
1995	144	506	109	149	33	104	31	120	83	.294	.431	.577
1996	158	517	122	159	42	129	40	151	76	.308	.461	.615
1997	159	532	123	155	40	101	37	145	87	.291	.446	.585
1998	156	552	120	167	37	122	28	130	92	.303	.438	.609

From the age of 25 to 33, Bonds had 4,539 at-bats. He hit 327 home runs—a home-run percentage of 7.2 percent. In other words, Bonds hit a home run every 13.9 at-bats. His highest homer total was in 1993, his first year with the Giants. That year he hit 46. His best ratio of home runs per at-bat was the strike-shortened 1994 season. Bonds hit 37 home runs in just 391 at-bats—a home-run percentage of 9.5 percent, that is, a homer every 10.6 at-bats.

Bonds's slugging percentage was typically at .600 or higher. His walk-to-strikeout ratio was solid, sometimes approaching 2 to 1. His batting average consistently approached or exceeded .300.

And if 1990 and 1991 are omitted, his on-base percentage always exceeded .425.

To be sure, through 1998 Bonds had superstar numbers but nothing that told us a 73-home-run season was probable. On the other hand, baseball has always had statistically anomalous seasons. When 5'6", 190-pound Hack Wilson hit 56 home runs and drove in 191 for the 1930 Chicago Cubs, there was no track record that would have foretold Wilson's enormous season. Wilson had never even hit 40 home runs in a single season before 1930. (He would never hit more than 23 home runs after 1930.) Wilson had never drawn as many as 80 walks in a season before 1930. He was walked 105 times in 1930. Wilson's 1930 slugging percentage (.723) was more than one hundred points higher than any other year of his career.

If Wilson were playing today and achieved the statistically anomalous success he achieved in 1930, would he be accused of steroid use? Of course he would.

What about Roger Maris? In 1961 Maris hit 61 home runs, breaking Babe Ruth's 1927 single-season record of 60. Before 1961, Maris hit 97 home runs in 1,873 at-bats. In other words, Maris hit a home run 5 percent of the time—a home run every 19.3 at-bats. From 1962 until he stopped playing in 1968, Maris hit 117 home runs in 2,638 at-bats. That's a home-run percentage of 4.4 percent, a home run every 22.5 at-bats. What happened in 1961? Maris hit 61 home runs in 590 at-bats for a home run every 9.67 at-bats and a home-run percentage of 10.3 percent.

So, was Maris's 1961 a greater statistical anomaly than Bonds's 2001? Barry Bonds's 2001 may stand as the single-greatest offensive season of any major league baseball player ever. Bonds hit 73 home runs in 476 at-bats. He doubled 32 times (twice as many as Maris hit in 1961). His batting average was .328. His slugging percentage was .863. Amazingly, Bonds hit a home run 15 percent of the time. He hit a home run every 6.5 at-bats.

In some ways, Maris's 1961 and Bonds's 2001 seasons are remarkably similar. Both players nearly doubled the home-run production that was statistically probable and expected. However, in some ways, Maris's 1961 was *more* statistically anomalous than Bonds's 2001. Before 2001, Bonds was already an established and selective power hitter who hit for average and sometimes drew twice as many walks as strikeouts. Before anyone ever accused Bonds of taking steroids, he hit more than 40 home runs in a season—three times. And he was on pace to reach 50 during the strike-shortened 1994 campaign (he wound up with 37 in 112 games).

In contrast, Maris never hit as many as 40 home runs, with the exception of his 61 in 1961. While it's true that Maris played during an era when pitching dominated, he never came close to hitting .300. Except for his home runs, Maris never generated a lot of extra-base hits. He had 34 doubles in 1962. But aside from that one year, he never managed to hit more than 21 doubles in a season. Maris's lifetime batting average was .260. Over the course of his career, he struck out a lot more than he walked.

Maris's astonishingly successful 1961 season is not proof that he cheated that year. It isn't even *evidence* that he cheated. Instead, the statistics show that Maris had confidence, got good pitches to hit, and was on a hot streak. He did nearly twice as well in the home-run department as we probably had a right to expect. But Roger Maris did not use steroids.

*

It isn't always home-run hitters who have statistically anomalous home-run years. Take Wade Boggs, for example. Boggs was a high-average, low-power hitter for the Boston Red Sox during most of his 18-year career. He was inducted into the Hall of Fame in 2005. Boggs's lifetime batting average was .328. He hit better than .355 in five separate seasons. In 1984, Boggs had 625 at-bats. He hit six home runs. In 1993, his first year with the New York Yankees, Boggs had 560 at-bats. He hit two home runs. Boggs had only two seasons in which he hit more than eight home runs. What happened in 1987, the year Boggs hit 24 home runs—more than twice as many as he ever hit in any other year? Boggs hit 24 home runs in 551 at-bats in that one year. The rest of his career involved 8,629 at-bats and just 94 home runs. Something happened in 1987, but it wasn't attributed to steroids.

3

Steroids

America's pastime is an outgrowth of bats and balls. Steroids are an outgrowth of balls—well, testicles, to be exact. The connection was established more than a hundred years ago. Endocrinology's "father," Arnold Adolf Berthold, experimented on roosters in 1849. Berthold castrated roosters and observed the loss of secondary sex characteristics, sex drive, and what Berthold perceived as aggression. He then re-implanted testicles in the birds' abdominal cavities and observed restoration of the secondary sex traits and behavior he would have typically associated with roosters, as opposed to hens. Almost 100 years later, in the 1930s, Dr. Charles Kochakian did experiments with castrated dogs that highlighted the tissue-building attributes of certain hormones.

By 1935 scientists had discovered that testosterone was the hormone responsible for masculinization. During World War II, German scientists were able to synthesize the first anabolic steroids. Some people even think the Germans gave anabolic steroids to their troops. Adolf Hitler himself is believed to have used anabolic steroids.

Testosterone—the classic male hormone—and synthetic steroids generate anabolic and androgenic effects. *Anabolic* refers to tissue building—the ability to build muscle. *Androgenic* refers to masculinizing effects, such as growth of facial hair, an attribute commonly associated with men. Anyone who uses steroids would love to be able to use a synthetic steroid that had significant anabolic effects and no androgenic effects. So far, however, it looks as if all anabolic steroids will always have some degree of androgenic effect.

Synthetic anabolic steroids are created by making small modifications to testosterone molecules. The modifications can give anabolic steroids certain characteristics, such as reduced masculinizing effects or slower processing rates.

Whether swallowed or injected, free testosterone should have little impact on the body because it is almost entirely degraded and inactivated during its first pass through the liver. To work the way athletes and doctors want them to work, anabolic steroids must be able to circulate through the bloodstream many times before they are degraded and inactivated by the liver. Through esterification or alkylation, however, testosterone can be chemically altered to be longer-lasting or effective even if it makes only one pass through the bloodstream before the liver inactivates it.

There is a long list of testosterone-derived synthetic steroids, including Dianabol. Dianabol, which was among the first anabolic steroids ever produced, is also called Dbol and is supposed to have been one of Arnold Schwarzenegger's favored steroids.

Other steroids are derived from 19-nortestosterone. These steroids include Deca Durabolin. Athletes call it Deca and usually speak of it with appreciation. The original "steroid guru," Dan Duchaine (who was once described as "a mixture of Andy Kaufman and Albert Einstein, with some Bart Simpson thrown in"), touted Deca in his *Underground Steroid Handbook*. Steroids derived from 19-nortestosterone are supposed to create few side effects and provide a high ratio of anabolic to androgenic impact.

Another class of steroids is derived from dihydrotestosterone. This group of steroids includes Winstrol (or Stanozolol), which is popular because it can be taken orally. Winstrol was the subject of a positive drug test that cost Canadian sprinter Ben Johnson his 100-meter gold medal at the 1988 Olympics in Seoul, Korea. Steroids derived from dihydrotestosterone are thought to generate relatively few side effects. While some have expressed concern about possible liver toxicity and joint problems, others insist that these steroids are relatively safe.

Some anabolic steroids are taken orally. Others are injected, typically intramuscularly. There are, however, other methods of ingestion, including transdermal patches and rectal suppositories. Medical professionals can use anabolic steroids to treat symptoms in men with unusually low testosterone levels.

Anabolic steroids work when received and processed in individual cells. Under normal circumstances a person's receptor sites tend to be saturated with natural testosterone molecules. This means that if you take anabolic steroids, work your desk job from 9:00 to 5:00, drive home, watch television until bedtime, and get up the next morning to repeat your routine, all those anabolic steroids do absolutely nothing. On the other hand, if you exercise like a maniac, your body will develop more receptor sites, and the anabolic steroids will work to help you build muscle. Or, at least that's the currently accepted theory.

For years, many believed steroids might facilitate water retention but do little else. Scientists doubted whether steroids could actually build muscle and increase strength. The scientific literature still leaves substantial room for doubt. Can steroids actually create muscle mass? Can steroids increase strength or quickness? Can steroids shorten recovery times or increase exercise stamina? Or, are athletes who take steroids—athletes who are willing to risk death to achieve their goals—already the type of people who are willing to work harder and longer in the weight room?

The truth is that no one really knows the extent of the muscle-building properties of steroids. Some studies support the theory that steroids can play a major role in muscle building. But some studies don't. In 1991 Dr. Glenn Braunstein said "great controversy surrounds the question of whether anabolic steroids actually increase strength and athletic performance."

Previously, in 1977, the American College of Sports Medicine stated that "there is no conclusive scientific evidence that extremely large doses of anabolic-androgenic steroids either aid or hinder athletic performance." But 10 years later that position was revised. The American College of Sports Medicine was willing to say that when combined with a proper diet, experienced weight trainers who used steroids could get an increase in strength that is "usually small and obviously not exhibited by all individuals." This was still far from a medical consensus that steroid use necessarily equals increased strength or speed for the user.

Because steroids work in conjunction with weight lifting (if they work at all), it is difficult to attribute muscle-mass gains specifically to steroids, on the one hand, versus the actual lifting of weights, on the other. One view of steroid efficacy is that they allow faster recoveries, so that users require shorter rest intervals between periods of exercise. In addition to the fact that steroids have been illegal in the United States since 1991, accurately assessing the impact of steroids is made even more difficult because of the well-known placebo effect. As early as 1972, studies demonstrated real strength gains in weight lifters who were told they had qualified to receive steroids (Dianabol) but who were actually given placebos. It is very possible that thousands of people walking around right this minute are thinking steroids helped them build muscle when in reality, their supplier was selling them fake steroids.

Science has no compelling answers yet. There are, of course, thousands of bodybuilders who believe the anabolic steroids facilitate creation of muscle mass. Quality studies that account for the variables and the placebo effect may be scarce, but there is no doubt that the general public believes steroids build muscle.

Human growth hormone (HGH), or somatotropin, is produced naturally by the pituitary gland. There was a time when people who wanted growth hormone had to get it from cadavers. Now, synthetic versions are available. HGH tells body cells to increase in size and to divide and reproduce more rapidly. Experts believe HGH can cause the body to decrease its utilization of carbohydrates and increase utilization of fats. So HGH is considered a strong anabolic—something that helps build muscle. Interestingly, however, some studies suggest that HGH does *not* increase strength. For example, in 2003 the *Journal of Applied Physiology* reported that subjects who received exogenous recombinant human growth hormone experienced improved lean body mass independent of their exercise levels. In contrast, the subjects' strength increases correlated directly to exercise. Perhaps HGH does more to reduce body fat than it does to increase strength.

There is enough anecdotal evidence to convince most people that steroids can increase muscle mass and strength in bodybuilders and football players. Still, when it comes to the question of whether steroids can help a baseball player who is looking for the curveball catch up to a Randy Johnson 98 mph fastball and pop it over the right-field fence, the jury is still out (to put it mildly).

Up until the 1990s the conventional wisdom in baseball was that lifting weights was counterproductive. Flexibility was king. Quickness was everything. Vision was critical. Big muscles would just get in the way. Ted Williams was the last man to hit over .400, and he was tall and relatively skinny (6'3" and about 180 pounds early in his career). Williams was no Ralph Garr, an outfielder with the Atlanta Braves in the 1970s, who regularly competed for the batting title but never hit more than 12 home runs in a season. Williams had power, too. When he hit .406 in 1941, Williams also pounded 37 home runs and 33 doubles. His on-base percentage was .553. His slugging percentage was .735. Williams walked 147 times and struck out only 27 times in 1941. Wow!

Those numbers spoke loudly—far louder than any weight room ever could. The year after he hit .406, he hit 36 home runs, drove in 137 runs, and batted .356. Because of his military service, Williams did not play in 1943, 1944, or 1945. His next at-bat came in 1946, his fifth year in the major leagues. Williams retired in 1960 with 521 home runs and a lifetime batting average of .344. He was a two-time Triple Crown winner, leading the league in home runs, batting average, and RBIs in 1942 and 1947.

After he enlisted, Williams served as a fighter pilot in the military, a patriotic duty that cost his baseball career three years to World War II and almost two years to the Korean War. His 20/10 vision helped him as a pilot, but it was an essential attribute that, together with skill and a scientific approach to hitting, made him one of the three best hitters in baseball history, along with Babe Ruth and Barry Bonds. Give Williams his five lost seasons, and his numbers would probably be comparable to Ruth's and Bonds's.

Before he ended his career in 1960, the "Splendid Splinter" had put on nearly 30 pounds. But the weight gain seemed to be the result of normal maturation and development. Williams wasn't really a weight lifter. And obviously, he was not on steroids. Up until the 1990s, baseball players just didn't lift weights. There were one or two notable exceptions, such as Ted Kluszewski, who played for the Cincinnati Reds in the late 1940s and 1950s. Big Ted was 6'2" and weighed 225 pounds—about the same size as Bonds. He lifted weights long before it was fashionable. In his day, Kluszewski was one of a kind. Ralph Kiner, the slugger who led the National League in home runs seven consecutive seasons from 1946 through 1952 (hitting 51 in 1947 and 54 in 1949), was more typical. As Kiner explained, "We had no weight room because lifting was considered the worst thing you could do." Kiner went on to say, "In my day, organizations commonly ordered players to not lift weights because they'd become too muscle-bound."

But in 1985, baseball started changing. José Canseco played in 29 games for the Oakland A's that year. The following season Canseco was a full-time outfielder who smashed 33 home runs. By 1988 the 6'4", 240-pound Canseco had become the founding member of baseball's 40-40 club—he hit 42 home runs and stole 40 bases. Canseco had proven weight lifting wasn't necessarily a bad thing for a baseball player—it could make some players much, much better.

In his 2005 "tell-all" book *Juiced,* Canseco claims to be the son of a hard-to-please and dominating father. He tells us how he promised his dying mother that he would become the greatest athlete in the world. Despite the sharing of such touching personal moments, *Juiced* is really a "tell-some" book, maybe even a "tell-a-little" book. Canseco says he was introduced to steroids in 1984.

As Canseco tells it, "Fortunately for me, I had a friend from high school (I'll call him Al) who knew a lot about steroids and had experimented with them." That's right, *Juiced* doesn't tell us who introduced Canseco to steroids. It doesn't tell us who supplied José's steroids. Instead, Canseco jumps right to the part about using steroids, and he says they worked for him and many other players.

Canseco says he was nervous at first, but after a while, it gets pretty easy to inject yourself with steroids. He explains that "steroids become like a friend." Canseco was an avid weight lifter. He started "with the light stuff," which he described as "basic testosterone, liquid form, combined with some Deca Durabolin." Canseco became very talented with the needle, and within a few years, he started earning "the chemist" nickname that would ultimately stick with him:

> As I experimented more, I started trying different categories
> of steroids. Different types do certain things to the muscles,

to the skin, the hair, the eyes, and your quick-muscle-twitch fibers. Every steroid played a different part. And when you combined them with growth hormones, the effect was just incredible.

Canseco says he soon graduated to Winstrol, Equipoise, Anadrone, and Anavar—to name a few. Some of these, such as Winstrol (Stanozolol) and Anavar (oxandrolone) are so-called 17-alkylated compounds that some see as potentially toxic, particularly to the liver. But nothing in this field is certain—some, for example, say Anavar is a mild and relatively "safe" steroid. As Canseco was entering major league baseball, Jim Rice was leaving. Rice played for the Red Sox from 1974 to 1989. He hit 382 home runs. In 1978 he had 46 home runs and 15 triples. He hit .315. Rice hit 39 home runs in three different years—1977, 1979, and 1983. Rice was an offensive force who certainly had strength and power. But he didn't lift weights. In fact, Rice bragged about never touching a weight during his 16 major league seasons. Rice's retirement coincided with the end of baseball's mythology that weight lifting would hurt performance.

While Canseco wants to take credit for single-handedly introducing the weight-lifting culture to baseball, many people believe he had a very improbable silent partner—Orrin Grant Hatch. Although he never made it to the major leagues (and apparently never lifted a weight), the conservative Republican from Utah (who had become an attorney in 1962 and a U.S. Senator in 1976) takes credit for the Dietary Supplement Health and Education Act, to this very day.

David Sills, presiding justice of Orange County, California's appellate court, explained the DSHEA like this:

> In 1994, Congress enacted the Dietary Supplement Health and Education Act. In plain political terms, the Dietary Supplement Health and Education Act was a slap at the

FDA (Food and Drug Administration). Consumers had feared the FDA was seeking to subject vitamins and minerals to the same expensive premarket approval processes that prescription drugs are subjected to.... Thus the core of the Dietary Supplement Health and Education Act was the exemption of dietary supplements from FDA premarket approval.

In *Juicing the Game*, Howard Bryant sees the DSHEA as a law that "shifted the burden of proof concerning a product's safety from the manufacturer to the [FDA]." According to Bryant, a company that manufactured supplements would no longer have "to prove its newest dietary supplements were safe." Instead, he says, "now the FDA, an often overburdened government agency, was forced to prove such products were not."

With Canseco touting the benefit of steroids to his teammates and players around the league and Hatch working to emasculate the FDA, baseball was about to enter the era of the long ball. To this very day, Canseco takes credit for introducing many players to the benefits of steroids. One Canseco disciple stands out from the rest: Mark McGwire. In his 1987 rookie year with the Oakland A's, the 6'5", 220-pound former USC Trojan hit 49 home runs. For a while, that seemed to be as good as it would get. In 1991 McGwire hit only 22 home runs in 483 at-bats. He struck out 116 times and his batting average was a mere .201.

But McGwire wasn't through. He rebounded to hit 42 home runs in 1992. Injuries stymied him in 1993 and 1994 (when he compiled a total of fewer than 220 at-bats and fewer than 20 home runs). But suddenly things turned around for Big Mac. He hit 39 home runs in 1995 and 52 (with a .312 batting average) in 1996. Despite being traded from the A's to the Cardinals, McGwire slammed 58 home runs in 1997. And then it was 1998.

*

Different kinds of athletes take different doses of steroids. A weight lifter's dosage will be substantially higher than a sprinter's. A constant steroid dosage is not an effective approach. The body has only so many receptors. So knowledgeable users "cycle," often in a pyramid style. The dose starts low, increases to a peak, and then is gradually reduced. Then the cycle repeats. According to Canseco, McGwire was friendly and liked to talk about steroids. As Canseco puts it, "One of the main things [he and McGwire] talked about was steroids—about how to tailor your doses and cycles to achieve the best results. We had access to the best steroids; it was like shopping from a high-end catalog."

Canseco says that beginning in 1988, he and McGwire were using steroids together. Canseco said he "injected Mark in the bathrooms at the Coliseum more times than I can remember." That same year, rumors of Canseco's steroid use hit the press. In Boston during the playoffs, fans started a "Steroids! Steroids!" chant. Canseco turned and flexed a bicep for the fans. The crowd reacted favorably.

Four years later Canseco was traded to the Texas Rangers. He figured the steroid rumors may have influenced the A's to trade him. Either way, the Rangers were happy to have Canseco—steroids were apparently not a problem for the Rangers (whose managing general partner was a guy named George W. Bush, a guy who ultimately was forced to move down into a government job). So Canseco says he met with some of his new teammates and taught them about steroids—teammates such as Juan Gonzalez, Ivan Rodriguez, and Rafael ("I have never used steroids. Period!") Palmeiro. Canseco contends that "I personally injected each of those three guys many times, until they became more familiar with how to use a needle and were able to do it themselves." Canseco says Bush regularly attended games and saw Gonzalez, Rodriguez, and Palmeiro "getting bigger before [his] eyes." But Bush never said a word.

Bush arguably was no different from other owners—owners who probably didn't care how or why home runs were being hit, as long as players with newly developed power kept producing and kept putting fans in the seats. But Bush may have had some personal attributes that made him particularly unlikely to try to do anything about the rampant steroid use Canseco says he had to have noticed. Bush may have been a bit overly eager to place professional athletes on a pedestal. He was, after all, head cheerleader when he was at Andover. So he may have learned to look up to athletes at an early age and in the worst possible way.

Then, at Yale and afterward, he is said to have exhibited the tendencies of an alcoholic (and some say he even used cocaine). If so, it may have been difficult for a person who had struggled with recreational drugs to even think about criticizing athletes who were hard-working and conscientious to the point of avoiding alcohol and tobacco—athletes who were using steroids to try to improve their strength and physical capabilities. Still, it is difficult to see Bush as a silent partner in a steroid conspiracy. No matter what Canseco says, it is easier to see the future president as someone who just didn't have a clue as to what was really going on.

Whether owners like Bush were coconspirators or not, it didn't take long for other players around the league to start asking Canseco for steroid advice. In his book Canseco writes:

> It wasn't like I did daily or weekly seminars in front of the whole ball team, standing up in front of them all in a white lab coat and holding up a laser pointer and telling them, "Today, we're going to learn about Deca and what it can do for you." But by then it was an open secret among players: if they wanted to know about steroids, they knew who to ask.

There was no going back. The weight-lifting culture was invading major league baseball. And Orrin Hatch's anti-FDA law was also having an impact. A mystery supplement was about to make its way around the major leagues.

*

September 29, 1996, was a historic day in baseball. A record Barry Bonds's father set 23 years earlier, in 1973, fell. In a single season, Bobby Bonds had once led off 11 games with a home run. But on September 29, 1996, Brady Anderson hit his 12th leadoff home run. Far more important, it was Anderson's 50th home run of the year. If Anderson had taken the day off and stopped at 49 home runs, the future of major league baseball may have been a bit different. But a manager who once had an improbable home-run season of his own, Davey Johnson, bowed to Anderson's wishes and let him play against the Toronto Blue Jays as the season was winding down. Anderson's 50th home run was the only run his Orioles scored that day.

In some ways, Anderson's 50-homer season was the most improbable ever. Anderson was big enough to hit home runs, at 6'1" and 185 pounds. But before 1996, the most home runs he ever hit in a season was 21. In fact, in eight seasons before 1996, Anderson hit a grand total of 72 home runs—72 home runs in 3,271 at-bats. Out of nowhere, in 1996 Anderson hit 50 home runs in 579 at-bats. Before 1996 he hit a home run every 45.4 at-bats. In 1996, Anderson hit a home run every 11.6 at-bats.

What was Anderson's secret? Creatine! Linford Christie won the gold medal in the 100 meters at the 1992 Olympics in Barcelona. He made it known that he used creatine before the Olympics. By 1993 creatine supplements were available in the United States. Anderson took creatine, and he lifted weights before and after games. During the off-season, Anderson lifted more weights. If creatine and weight lifting could turn a leadoff hitter who had never hit .275 and never hit 25 home runs into a .297 hitter who slammed 50 home runs in a single season, what could they do for a power hitter?

Athletes can take creatine in a tablet form, or they can mix powdered creatine with liquid to make it drinkable. Creatine helps the athlete's body go from inaction to action—quickness. Quickness depends on adenosine triphosphate (ATP). The theory is that creatine rapidly regenerates ATP. This expedites the fast-twitch muscle fibers that rely on energy reserves, rather than oxygen. By maximizing ATP recycling, creatine is thought to be able to increase the duration of intense exercise that an athlete can tolerate. This means that a person taking creatine can theoretically engage in harder, longer, and more intense workouts.

Creatine might not do much to help an endurance athlete such as Lance Armstrong, but it might have greatly benefited Anderson. Creatine is *not* a steroid. It exists naturally in common foods, such as beef. Whether creatine actually increases strength and quickness is, however, debatable. Relatively few studies of its efficacy have been performed, and none are particularly convincing.

Nevertheless, by the mid-1990s creatine was as common in major league clubhouses as chewing tobacco used to be. Just a few years earlier weight lifting had been viewed as bizarre and inappropriate. Now it was the norm. Every major league team had a weight room. Some teams, such as the Oakland A's and the St. Louis Cardinals, even supplied creatine and protein powders for their players.

Still, outside of baseball and athletics in general, few people were familiar with creatine. An Associated Press writer named Steve Wilstein single-handedly opened everyone's eyes during the summer of 1998. The Magic Season—1998—was the year Mark McGwire and Sammy Sosa "saved" baseball. The strike that had canceled the 1994 World Series had created a lingering negativity. But with McGwire and Sosa slamming home runs at a record pace, people who had vowed not to pay any attention to the spoiled, overpaid egomaniacs who played baseball for a living started watching again.

Wilstein had been assigned to cover McGwire as he was closing in on Maris's record. One day, as Wilstein and other reporters were standing around McGwire's locker, Wilstein was taking notes on everything he saw. That day Wilstein saw one small thing the other reporters missed—a brown bottle labeled with a word he didn't understand: Androstenedione. Wilstein called a doctor friend and asked about androstenedione (andro). Wilstein was told that andro was a testosterone precursor that could be bad for the heart. He soon learned that the National Football League considered andro a steroid, and it was banned in the NFL. When Wilstein asked the Cardinals whether McGwire was taking andro, he received a negative response. A spokesperson explained that "he [McGwire] doesn't even know how to spell it." That was a lie. Well, technically it may have been true. It's possible that like most of us, McGwire might have trouble spelling androstenedione; but any implication that he was unfamiliar with the stuff was pure fantasy.

Wilstein's story hit the papers on August 21, 1998. McGwire had confessed to using andro and said he'd been taking creatine for about four years. The article mentioned that Sosa used creatine but not andro. The story also quoted Andres Galarraga—the slugger who retired with 399 home runs, 44 of which were hit in 1998—as saying he would be "scared" to take a drug like andro.

Galarraga had good reason to be concerned. Andro is a testosterone precursor, but it also facilitates development of the female hormone estrogen. Some studies suggest that andro does no more to build muscle than a simple placebo does. But andro's attributes are linked to possible increased risks of certain estrogen-related cancers and heart disease.

Wilstein should get credit for pushing Major League Baseball a little closer toward responding to a growing problem. However, the Cardinals' manager, former attorney Tony LaRussa, challenged Wilstein for invading McGwire's privacy. It was a classic example of "blame the messenger" and change the subject. The players, and even the press, vigorously defended McGwire. The commissioner's office started to investigate andro. Slowly. And Donald Fehr, head of the Players Association, saw this as a DSHEA-related problem, where Orrin Hatch's law allowed a steroid to be treated as a food supplement. (The federal government finally made andro illegal in 2004.)

Canseco offers a unique perspective on McGwire's use of andro. Canseco thinks McGwire might have left the andro bottle in plain sight on purpose. Since andro was legal, it offered McGwire a cover. It gave him the ability to blame his new size and strength on andro, rather than illegal steroids. In addition, Canseco theorized that McGwire might have been planning to blame any failed steroid test on andro. According to Canseco:

> Mark was an experienced steroid user, as I know firsthand. His physique speaks for itself. And he knows as well as I do that if you were taking steroids, you don't need androstene-dione. McGwire using andro would've been like a hospital patient on morphine asking for an aspirin. It just doesn't make any sense.... I don't believe Mark McGwire was even taking andro. Why would he? That bottle of andro was just sitting in his locker; that doesn't mean he actually used it. To me, it seems more likely that the whole thing was an illusion. I'm virtually certain that Mark created the andro controversy as a distraction.

The treatment (or, more accurately, abuse) Wilstein received for "outing" McGwire is inconsistent with Canseco's theory. But it is consistent with Canseco's belief that McGwire was a very smart cheater. In any event, within a few weeks the andro furor had died down. The home-run race continued. McGwire ended up with 70 home runs, and Sosa hit 66. Those numbers were off the charts. It was a high point for baseball. Or was it?

*

Ken Caminiti was a solid hitter and an excellent third baseman during his 15 major league seasons. In 2002 Caminiti became the first player to publicly admit that he'd used real steroids. Caminiti revealed that he had in fact used steroids during his 1996 MVP season (40 HR, 130 RBI, .326). If Caminiti's confession had stopped there, it might not have been so damaging. But Caminiti also said, "It's no secret what's going on in baseball. At least half the guys are using [steroids]. They talk about it. They joke about it with each other."

Although anabolic steroids were illegal, Major League Baseball seemed to have no official rules against them and no testing program— a little problem that led to the awkward day in March 2005, when Mark McGwire, Sammy Sosa, Rafael Palmeiro, Curt Schilling, Frank Thomas, and José Canseco got to talk to the United States Congress. In response to questions from our country's top lawmakers, Sosa denied using steroids. McGwire pathetically refused to answer questions, repeatedly noting that he was "not here to talk about the past." What was he there to talk about, the weather? The numbers for next week's lottery drawing? It was a farce.

Canseco candidly admitted to using steroids. And he said he had a hard time believing some of the other testimony—testimony that made it sound like Canseco was the only major league player who ever used steroids.

Palmeiro managed to make McGwire look even worse. He pointed an index finger right at our congressional bigwigs and proclaimed that "I have never used steroids. Period!" The flat-out denial made

McGwire's evasive non-answers look like a tacit (or perhaps not so tacit) admission.

But, to the extent it was possible, Palmeiro was about to sink even lower than McGwire. According to Canseco, Palmeiro was one of his Texas Rangers teammates he had personally injected with steroids. But everyone in baseball said Canseco was making all this stuff up— he allegedly had financial problems and needed to say something outlandish to sell his book. Palmeiro had to be telling the truth—the hardest drug he'd ever taken was Pfizer's Viagra. He hit his 551 home runs at that point in his career the old-fashioned way, without any help from Canseco and steroids. His testimony was emphatic. Canseco was a liar. Palmeiro was a hero.

Not so fast. It would actually be funny if it wasn't so sad. The publicity surrounding the steroid controversy had forced baseball's owners to implement (and the players union to accept) a modest testing program. And a few months after he pointed his finger at the world and solemnly swore that he had *never* used a steroid, Palmeiro became the first high-profile player to be suspended for a positive steroid test. Suddenly, Canseco's credibility level seemed to skyrocket. It looked as if the only legitimate finger-pointing was Canseco's pointing the finger at Palmeiro. Palmeiro backed away from the "I have never used steroids. Period!" Now he sounded lawyerly, noting that he did not take steroids "intentionally or knowingly." If Canseco was really injecting his butt full of stuff, what did Palmeiro think it was? Flu vaccine?

When professional baseball players start using legalese we know trouble is on the horizon. Palmeiro's positive steroid test meant that Caminiti and Canseco had to be taken seriously, even if they were exaggerating. Whether baseball's steroid users were limited to a relative handful of bad apples or 20 percent of the players, the issue had to be confronted.

And baseball's most dominant player would have to be pursued even more vigorously.

4

The People versus Bonds

In the court of public opinion Barry Bonds may already stand convicted. Particularly because Bonds has treated so many people so badly, many people are ready and more than willing to believe that Bonds regularly and knowingly used steroids. Many people want to believe Bonds would not hold the single-season home-run record and could not have eclipsed Hank Aaron's all-time home-run record, except for his rampant steroid use.

But many people who have convicted Bonds in their own minds have not yet closely studied the evidence. It isn't their fault. No one is out there compiling evidence to defend Bonds. But plenty of contrary evidence exists. And there are plenty of problems with the evidence that has been compiled against Bonds. For example, we can start with the glaring absence of direct evidence. While José Canseco has stepped forward to acknowledge injecting steroids into Mark McGwire, there is no similar eyewitness account by an accomplice when it comes to Bonds.

So what exactly is this mountain of evidence that has convinced so many that Bonds used steroids, that he did so knowingly, and that the steroids are responsible for all those home runs? The most vigorous effort to prosecute Bonds in the court of public opinion comes from an unlikely source—two *San Francisco Chronicle* writers, one of whom was actually Barry Bonds's codefendant in a defamation lawsuit a podiatrist filed against Bonds, Mark Fainaru-Wada, and others. In their 2006 book, *Game of Shadows*, Fainaru-Wada and Lance Williams make a venomous and sustained attack against Bonds. In addition to Bonds, *Shadows* villainizes Marion Jones, Tim Montgomery, and a few other athletes. Next to Bonds, however, *Shadows* aims most of its animosity at both Greg Anderson, Bonds's boyhood acquaintance and personal trainer, and Victor Conte, a onetime bass player for Tower of Power, who went on to found BALCO, the Bay Area Laboratory Co-Operative, which is thought to have distributed designer steroids to professional track athletes, football players, and baseball players.

In a book that spans more than 260 pages, Williams and Fainaru-Wada relentlessly attack Bonds. They start by theorizing that Bonds was jealous of McGwire and Sosa in 1998—the year both of them hit more home runs than Roger Maris hit in 1961. From there, *Shadows* misses almost no opportunity to belittle Bonds as a person, as a player, as a father, and as a teammate. (Yes, Bonds deserves much of that criticism.) Along the way *Shadows* compiles a list of what is supposed to serve as proof of Bonds's steroid use. This evidentiary list is populated with everything from secret recordings that appear to have been obtained illegally to the recollections of a jilted lover.

We already knew Bonds was hated by many baseball fans and much of the press. And *Shadows* reminds us of all that. It also lists the evidence that supposedly proves (1) that Bonds used steroids, (2) that he did so knowingly, and (3) that steroids are responsible for Bonds's success as a hitter. But if a fair-minded person looks at that so-called evidence, it is hard to see it as anything but surprisingly weak. The "proof" of Bonds's alleged steroid use starts with the argument that Bonds just *looks* guilty.

Looks

Many people who believe Bonds used steroids say the way Bonds looks is itself evidence of significant steroid use. From the pages of *Shadows* we learn that "to some experts, the changes in Bonds's body over the course of his career constitute persuasive evidence of steroid use." They say Bonds gained 43 pounds over a 17-year period—an average of 2.5 pounds per year. Because the weight gain is said to consist primarily of muscle, as opposed to fat, it is viewed as evidence of significant steroid use.

But it isn't just the weight gain. The *Shadows* authors and others believe that Bonds's head or skull has grown significantly over the years. As *Shadows* tell us:

> [T]he Barry Bonds of 2001 didn't look anything like the lithe, young Pirate who used to knock the ball into the gap, accelerate as he took the turn at first base, and fly into second for a double. Actually, with his massive, pumped-up musculature, his shaven head, his fierce game face, and the diamond earring dangling from his left ear, the Bonds of 2001 didn't look like any baseball player you had ever seen. Bonds looked like a WWE wrestler, or a toy superhuman action figure, but not a ballplayer.

For highly regarded journalists, the *Shadows* authors seem unusually fixated on looks. The book is especially harsh toward people the authors dislike. For example, Fainaru-Wada and Williams criticized a story that appeared in *Muscle and Fitness* magazine because it portrayed Bonds's trainer, Greg Anderson, "as more of the nutritional technician than a tattooed gym rat."

The *Shadows* authors never try to hide the extreme contempt they harbor toward Conte, BALCO's founder. More than once, *Shadows* actually refers to Conte's "cheesy mustache." While they hope to make the reader hate Conte, their attacks are so inapposite that they backfire. *Shadows* lays it on so thick that some readers find themselves feeling sorry for Conte.

We should remember that the *Shadows* authors aren't the only ones who seem to think that they can prove Bonds took steroids based on the way he looks. No less of an authority than Canseco himself has said, "It's not that hard to tell when someone is using steroids. You just have to trust your eyes. If someone adds a huge amount of muscle and does it quickly, you know he's using steroids. There's just no other way to do it."

But trusting our eyes isn't always so easy. Although some saw a Bonds that was getting huge, some seemed to think Bonds was actually shrinking during the middle of his supposed steroid binge. As Jeff Pearlman put it in *Love Me, Hate Me: Barry Bonds and the Making of an Antihero*, "At the start of spring training [2002], Bonds reported to camp looking significantly smaller than he had toward the end of the 2001 season, when he weighed a reported 228 pounds."

So whose eyes should we trust? The ones who thought Bonds was growing by leaps and bounds, or the ones who thought he was getting a little smaller during the middle of his alleged steroid heyday?

While many of us think looks can be deceiving, to the *Shadows* authors, looks were critical and important evidence, and nothing was off-limits. Nothing was too small to be noticed. For example, Bonds was allegedly shaving his head because the steroids had caused his hair to fall out. (Was Michael Jordan on steroids, too?) And Bonds's "head itself seemed to be getting larger, and the plates of his skull bones stood out in bold relief." *Shadows* even sees the pimples on Bonds's back as yet another telltale sign of steroid use. While pimples or hair loss may be possible side effects, they are not conclusive proof of steroid use.

There are a lot of people who think they can just look at someone and know whether or not the person they're looking at is a steroid user. Turk Wendell pitched in the major leagues for 11 seasons. Wendell was a journeyman relief pitcher who ended his career with 33 saves and a 3.93 ERA. Apparently, Wendell also fancies himself as something of a steroid expert. In 2004, when addressing the question of whether Bonds used steroids, his take was in the affirmative, concluding that "it's clear just seeing his body."

Although the way Bonds looks is thought to be the most compelling evidence, there is more. Some say Bonds's success as a hitter proves he used steroids.

Statistics

Maybe Mark Twain said it best when he said, "There are three kinds of lies: lies, damned lies, and statistics." To the *Shadows* authors, statistics left no doubt: "At an age when his father's baseball skills had begun to erode badly, Bonds's drug use would make him a better hitter than he had been at any time in his career—and, perhaps, the best hitter of all time."

Arguing that Bonds started taking steroids after he watched Sosa and McGwire devastate the record book in 1998, Fainaru-Wada and Williams conclude that "the transformation that Barry Bonds achieved through the use of performance-enhancing drugs is reflected in his batting statistics." They point out that four of Bonds's five best seasons came after he turned 35. They say that, oddly, five of the six times Bonds hit 45 or more home runs came after 1999, when he was allegedly using performance-enhancing drugs.

They go on to say Bonds's ratio of home runs per at-bat dramatically improved from 1999 to 2004, "after steroids." During those years Bonds hit a home run every 8.5 at-bats. Before that, his best year was 1994, when he hit a home run every 10.6 at-bats. Noting the increase in home runs per at-bat, batting average, and walks, *Shadows* concludes that "at what should have been the end of his baseball career, Bonds became a significantly better hitter than at any time in his life."

Apparently assuming that no person who wasn't using steroids could be anywhere near as statistically capable as Babe Ruth, the *Shadows* authors argue that the "post-steroids Bonds also became one of the greatest hitters of all time." They argue that Bonds's 2001 season was the second-best offensive season any player has ever had—"second only to Babe Ruth's 1921 season, when the New York Yankees star hit .378 with 171 RBI."

Looking back to seasons like Babe Ruth's 1921, Lou Gehrig's 1936, and Rogers Hornsby's 1922, the *Shadows* authors argue that Bonds must have been using steroids because most statistically comparable seasons had been attained by players who were several years younger than Bonds was when he was putting up huge numbers. Some of the stats they identify as meaningful are:

Player	Yr.	Age	Avg.	HR	RBI	Slg.
Ruth	1921	26	.378	59	171	.846
Foxx	1932	24	.364	58	169	.749
Gehrig	1936	33	.354	49	152	.696
Bonds	2001	36	.328	73	137	.863
Bonds	2004	39	.362	45	101	.812

To assess and compare one player's season against another's, *Shadows* relies on Lee Sinins's calculations using a version of Bill James's "runs created" formula. This approach omits some pretty impressive seasons offensive players have had over the years. Among the unmentioned:

Player	Yr.	Age	Avg.	HR	RBI	Slg.
H. Wilson	1930	30	.356	56	191	.723
T. Williams	1941	22	.406	37	120	.735
W. Mays	1965	34	.317	52	112	.645
L. Walker	1997	30	.366	49	130	.720

Hack Wilson's 1930 season was still arguably the most productive ever. His 191 runs batted in stand as a record Bonds never approached. By hitting over .400 in 1941, Ted Williams assured himself a position of incomparability. When Willie Mays hit 52 home runs and batted

.317 in 1965, the National League's earned-run average was 3.54 (compared to 4.44 in 2007). As a whole, National League pitchers struck out more than two batters for every one that they walked that year. Mays's 52 home runs were 13 more than the closest runner-up (Willie McCovey hit 39; no other major league player even hit 35). And Larry Walker came close to winning the Triple Crown in 1997.

There is no doubt that Bonds performed *very* well from 2000 through 2004. To some, Bonds's statistical success is enough to prove steroid use. While *Shadows* may not go that far, it emphasizes that Bonds was much better from 1999 to 2004 than he was earlier in his career. The book sees the success as powerful evidence of steroid use beginning in 1998.

Statistically, only Ruth was more dominating than Bonds. After Bonds allegedly started using steroids, his batting average increased by 38 points. In addition, *Shadows* emphasizes that Bonds hit more home runs after turning 35 than "any of the game's great sluggers." This, again, is viewed as evidence of steroid use.

Sean Forman, the proprietor of Baseball-Reference.com, did a study for the *San Francisco Chronicle* that measured offensive performance by combining on-base percentage with slugging percentage (OPS). Not surprisingly, the study concluded that Bonds had amassed the five best consecutive seasons in the history of baseball between 2000 and 2004. Again, success is equated with steroid use.

Bill Jenkinson is a talented baseball writer and historian who has painstakingly tracked the distance of home runs Bonds and other players have hit over the years. If you've hit more than 300 major league home runs (and really, who hasn't?), Jenkinson probably has a "power performance curve" reflecting the distance of your home runs. (Apparently, long fly balls don't count, except when Jenkinson is arguing that Ruth would have hit 100 home runs in a year if he played today.)

According to Jenkinson, "Every single slugger I've ever evaluated peaked for distance in their mid- to late 20s." Jenkinson identifies one exception—Barry Bonds. "It's ridiculous," Jenkinson says. "From age 36 on he starts hitting the ball farther and farther." Jenkinson tells us that up until 2000, Bonds generally hit home runs that traveled 435 to 440 feet. After he turned 36, however, Bonds routinely hit 480-foot shots. Jenkinson concludes "that is not humanly possible." It cannot be done by even the most amazing athletic specimen of all time. "Unless," Jenkinson argues, "that specimen is cheating."

Jeff Novitzky

Jeff Novitzky wanted Bonds, and he wanted him bad. Novitzky worked as a special agent for the Internal Revenue Service's Criminal Investigation unit (IRS CI). In his mid-30s, Novitzky carried a gun and was described as part IRS auditor and part federal narcotics officer. Novitzky is central to the case against Bonds. Some might say Novitzky *is* the case against Bonds.

A dedicated public servant, Novitzky apparently volunteered his evenings to routinely sift through BALCO's trash. His quest for Bonds was that intense. On Monday evenings, Novitzky would drive to the Bay Area Laboratory Co-Operative in Burlingame, arriving at about 10:00 in the evening. Novitzky emptied two plastic trash cans and a recycling bin BALCO used into his own car, drove to a nearby office parking lot, and sorted through BALCO's garbage.

Novitzky was pleased when he found things that might be incriminating. The *Shadows* authors highlight the night Novitzky found a torn email printout that he interpreted as a price sheet for specially made substances, along with descriptions of proper administration. It said:

> Invisible "BT"—injectable…the more genetically gifted the athlete the more BT works.

Invisible "NP"—injectable…works best on a high-protein diet.

Invisible "HD"—cream…works best taken three times per day.

Novitzky even found notes from various athletes to BALCO's founder, Conte. One note was from a shot put champion, Kevin Toth. The note said, "Vic, you are the man." Another note was from Regina Jacobs, a distance runner who set a world record in the 1,500 meters as she was nearing age 40. Jacobs's note said, "All that I have accomplished this season would not have been possible without your support."

Novitzky kept digging. He found FedEx receipts with Greg Anderson's name on them. Novitzky knew Anderson as Barry Bonds's boyhood acquaintance who was now serving as Bonds's personal trainer. Novitzky was getting warmer.

Novitzky even found paperwork that mentioned several baseball players, some of whom had been Bonds's teammates, including Benito Santiago, Marvin Benard, Armando Rios, Jeremy Giambi, and Gary Sheffield.

Novitzky's biggest night was on March 3, 2003. During that particular investigation, Novitzky found a pill jar for a diet drug, a bottle that was labeled with the name of what purported to be a Russian anabolic dietary supplement, and four empty pill sheets of a female fertility drug known as Clomid. Clomid is thought to increase testosterone levels in men and prevent breast enlargement, or *gynocomastia*, which can be a problem for some steroid users.

And—for the very first time—Novitzky also found documents relating to Bonds. There was a fax from Conte to *Muscle and Fitness* magazine describing Bonds's weight training and nutrition program. There was also a document suggesting that Bonds's blood had been sent to a lab for steroid testing. The documents indicated that Bonds's sample had been sent to LabOne in Kansas. But subsequent documents identified the name on the test paperwork as "Greg Anderson," rather than Bonds. Was this a smoking gun that proved a cover-up?

In 2000 the San Mateo County sheriff's office had tried to get Anderson to sell steroids to an undercover officer at the World Gym where Anderson did much of his training. That operation was conducted more than a year after Bonds allegedly started using Anderson-provided steroids. The sheriffs, however, were unable to make a buy from Anderson.

By late 2002 Novitzky's team was closely monitoring BALCO. For example, agents observed Anderson, along with Randy Velarde, visiting BALCO. Velarde was in the last of his 16 major league seasons. He had a lifetime batting average of .276 and hit exactly 100 home runs during his career. In 2002 he hit .226 for the Oakland A's, with two home runs. (If Anderson was giving Velarde steroids, they were not working very well.)

Novitzky's team was following Conte. Agents watched Conte go into a Wells Fargo Bank and make a $2,000 cash withdrawal. When Conte took the money he told the teller that he would "see you tomorrow." This was enough to make Novitzky believe Conte was a drug dealer who was using cash to minimize the evidentiary paper trail (and his tax obligations).

Novitzky was also sifting through BALCO's medical waste. He found empty vials of EPO (erythropoietin, a drug thought to enhance endurance by increasing red blood cell counts), used syringes, and empty vials that were thought to have contained human growth hormone (HGH) and bacteriostatic water (which could be used to dilute or reconstitute powdered forms of HGH or "fake" HGH). Still with nothing to directly link Bonds and steroids, Novitzky turned to undercover infiltration during 2003. He assigned Iran White, a muscular California Bureau of Narcotics Enforcement officer, to get close to Anderson. White wore a wire and started working out with Anderson at Bay Area Fitness.

Anderson certainly bragged about his relationship with Bonds. And White got close enough to Anderson to be invited to Pac Bell Park. But White never obtained any evidence linking Bonds to steroids.

Meanwhile, in July 2003, Don Catlin and his UCLA colleagues identified a substance that was related to steroids known as gestrinone and trenbolone. This was a new steroid that Catlin's lab's scientific director, Michael Sekera, called tetrahydrogestrinone, or THG. It is more commonly known as "the Clear." Four BALCO clients tested positive for THG. The shot-putter, Toth; hammer throwers John McEwen and Melissa Price; and the runner, Jacobs, all tested positive.

Still, there was little, if anything, tying Bonds to steroids. There was, however, an interesting theory, and it went something like this. In 1998 Bonds watched McGwire hit 70 home runs and Sosa hit 66. Sosa and McGwire had the entire country watching them, rooting for them. Bonds got jealous. He had home-run envy. After the 1998 season ended, Bonds hooked up with Anderson and started taking Winstrol (Stanozolol). Then Anderson put Bonds on an injectable steroid, Deca Durabolin. Eventually, Anderson put Bonds on human growth hormone. Anderson kept all the steroids for Bonds. Bonds paid Anderson in cash, and sporadically at that.

The theory goes on to suggest that after the 2000 season ended, Bonds decided to break McGwire's single-season home-run record. So Anderson hooked up with Conte and BALCO. The BALCO connection allegedly gave Bonds access to a more thoughtful steroid program that ultimately included HGH, testosterone, insulin, so-called Mexican beans, trenbolone, the Clear, the Cream, and Clomid. No real paper trail could be found because Bonds didn't pay for the steroids with money. Instead, he volunteered to help promote BALCO's perfectly legal supplement, ZMA, a mineral compound that includes zinc and magnesium.

Armed with boatloads of suspicion and some interesting theories, but with virtually no actual evidence, Novitzky had to do something big. On September 3, 2003, a team of about 25 agents and experts from several different agencies swarmed BALCO's offices. They arrived during the lunch hour. Novitzky took Conte to a conference room, where there was one observer but no tape recorder. According to Novitzky, Conte voluntarily spoke to him for upward of three hours. Novitzky says Conte explained his distribution of the Clear and the Cream and specifically implicated 27 athletes. One of those 27 was, according to Novitzky, Barry Lamar Bonds. Novitzky says Conte told him that Greg Anderson had brought in several baseball players before the start of the 2003 season (which was to be the first season with Major League Baseball steroid testing in place). Conte supposedly told Novitzky that BALCO had supplied Bonds with the Clear and the Cream and that Bonds used those substances "on a regular basis."

Then Novitzky turned his attention to Anderson. They searched Anderson's home and found a syringe with traces of THG along with other syringes, empty vials, and diuretic pill sheets. Anderson answered a few questions, telling the agents that he had started working with professional athletes in 1997. He reportedly told Novitzky and his team that he gave the Cream and the Clear to professional athletes and sent some baseball players testosterone and HGH via FedEx. Anderson said he got HGH and testosterone from AIDS patients in the San Francisco area, and he admitted giving HGH to Bobby Estalella, Rios, and Santiago.

While they were searching Anderson's home, agents found file folders with the names of baseball players. There was a folder for Bonds.

The "Leaked" Grand Jury Testimony

Bonds testified before a grand jury that was investigating BALCO. Oddly, it was Novitzky who drove Bonds to the federal building on December 4, 2003. The day started poorly for Bonds and his attorney, Michael Rains. Almost immediately, prosecutors reneged on a deal to allow Rains to review documents before Bonds testified. This certainly made it look as if Bonds was a primary target of the investigation and that prosecutors would be all too happy if they could ultimately pursue perjury charges against Bonds.

Like other grand jury witnesses, Bonds had to take the witness stand without legal assistance and face two experienced prosecutors. Rains had to wait outside. Jeffrey D. Nedrow had passed the bar exam in 1992 (after graduating from UCLA School of Law), and now he was pitching questions to the best hitter in the world. Bonds immediately complained that Nedrow was confusing. Nedrow held his ground, outlining the immunity agreement that would allow Bonds to be prosecuted for perjury but not for taking illegal substances. Bonds explained that he'd known Anderson since both were boys, and he described how Anderson had introduced him to BALCO. Nedrow's boss, Ross Nadel, was soon lending a helping hand in the witness examination. Nadel had graduated from Santa Clara University School of Law back in 1979, and he had already tried about 70 cases. Bonds's legal experience was pretty much confined to one case, but it was a big one—his highly publicized divorce that went all the way to California's Supreme Court.

Now, Nadel and Nedrow started showing Bonds various documents that were thought to tie Bonds to steroids. They asked about the Clear and the Cream. Bonds answered:

> At the end of 2002, 2003 season, when I was going through—
> my dad died of cancer.... I was fatigued, just needing recov-
> ery now, and this guy says, "Try this cream, try this cream,"

he said. And Greg came to the ballpark and said, you know, "This will help you recover." And he rubs some cream on my arm…gave me some flaxseed oil, man it's like, "Whatever, dude." And I was at the ballpark, whatever. I don't care. What's lotion going to do for me? How many times I heard that "this is going to rub into you and work?" Let him be happy, we're friends, you know?

The prosecutors showed Bonds a vial that was thought to have contained the Clear. Bonds said the vial was for flaxseed oil. Bonds said he'd taken the oil by placing a couple of drops under his tongue. Some have insisted this proves Bonds used the Clear and that he did so knowingly. After all, they say, direct oral ingestion is no way to take flaxseed oil.

Bonds explained:

And I was like, to me, it didn't even work. You know me, I'm 39 years old. I'm dealing with pain. All I want is the pain relief, you know? And you know, to recover, you know, night games to day games. That's it. And I didn't think the stuff worked. I was like, "Dude, whatever," but he's my friend.... I never asked Greg. When he said it was flaxseed oil, I just said, "Whatever." It was in the ballpark…in front of everybody. I mean, all the reporters, my teammates. I mean, they all saw it. I didn't hide it. I didn't hide it.... You know, trainers come up to me and say, "Hey Barry, try this."

So the prosecutors returned to the documents that had been confiscated from Conte and Anderson. Did a reference to the letter *G* mean that Bonds was taking human growth hormone? Bonds simply explained that he didn't "know what *G* is." Bonds also apparently volunteered that he'd never injected himself with drugs.

When asked about paperwork that was thought to have reflected testing Bonds's blood, Bonds said he knew nothing about the paperwork. Asked about a document that referred to a $1,500 charge for HGH, Bonds responded that "Greg and I are friends. I never paid Greg for anything. I gave Greg money for his training me." Anticipating the subsequent questioning and trying to help move the process along, Bonds volunteered, "You're going to bring up documents and more documents. I have never seen anything written by Greg Anderson on a piece of paper."

Nadel asked Bonds about a bottle and a document that referred to depo testosterone. Bonds explained that he had "never ever seen this bottle or any bottle…that says depo testosterone."

Prosecutors asked about Clomiphene—an antiestrogen that might help a steroid user who was coming off a cycle. Bonds replied, "I've never heard of it." What about EPO (erythropoietin, the endurance booster)? Bonds replied, "I couldn't even pronounce it." Modafinil, the stimulant? Again, Bonds said, "I've never heard of it."

The prosecutors asked Bonds about a document that said, "Barry 12-2-02 T, 1CC G—Pee." Did this mean that on December 2, 2002, Bonds had been taking testosterone and human growth hormone, and then given Anderson a urine sample? Bonds answered the way you might expect a person who feared perjury charges to answer: "*T* could mean anything. *G* could mean anything. And *pee* could probably mean anything."

But the veteran prosecutors didn't give up. They asked Bonds about a medical report describing what was believed to be Bonds's testosterone levels. "I wouldn't even understand it anyway," Bonds said. "So they wouldn't talk to me about that."

Prosecutors asked about a calendar that was thought to refer to Clomid, the female fertility drug. Bonds responded, "I've never had a calendar with him, never had anything." So they asked if

Anderson had given Bonds insulin. "Insulin?" Bonds asked. "I'm not a diabetic."

More than three hours of questioning, and those were the highlights. It's safe to say the grand jury session was not exactly *SportsCenter* material. Maybe it wasn't even good enough for *Court TV*.

Kimberly Bell

To the people who are out to get Barry Bonds, Kimberly Bell is as good as it gets. To the *Shadows* authors, "No one was in better position to note Bonds's transformation and its side effects than Kimberly Bell." They depict her as "pretty and intuitive"—a virtual saint.

Bonds met Bell in 1994, as he was divorcing his first wife, Sun. Bell had a friend who "knew some ballplayers." She met Bonds in the players' parking lot before a Giants-Expos game. The divorce litigation was getting to Bonds, and he told Bell he never wanted to marry again. That was fine with Bell.

They started dating. At first, Bell kept her apartment and her job at Adobe. According to *Shadows*, Bonds was generous. When her car broke down, he bought her a new Toyota 4Runner. When she needed money, Bonds would give her $5,000 or more in cash—money he earned signing autographs or selling autographed balls, bats, and memorabilia. In 1996, when she needed bigger breasts, Bonds bought her a matching set.

Bell started going to baseball games. She particularly enjoyed the road trips, where she often stayed in the Giants' hotel. In 1997 Bonds told her he had met a woman named Liz Watson in Montreal, and Watson was staying at his condominium. Bell didn't bother to protest. Instead of beginning to look for a man who might be a slightly more permanent fixture in her life, she continued seeing Bonds.

Then, early in 1998, Bonds told Bell he was going to marry Watson. That bothered Bell, at least a little. When Bonds returned from his honeymoon with Watson, the affair with Bell resumed. While

Bonds may not regret the affair, he did a few things he probably does regret.

First, Bonds liberally left messages on Bell's answering machine. Bell kept the tapes. In the best of the messages (from Bonds's perspective), Bonds just sounded like an imbecile. In the worst, Bonds sounded like someone who belonged in jail. For example, the *Shadows* authors say that in one message Bonds left on Bell's machine he said, "If I don't know where you are, then a niggah's going to kill somebody. Good-bye."

Then, during spring training in 2001, Bonds took Bell for a romantic dinner at Morton's in Arizona. Afterward, Bell said she would love to live in Arizona. Bonds decided to make that happen—a big mistake. Bell says Bonds planned to give her cash generated from card shows until Bell had enough money to make a down payment on a house. The cash, which allegedly wasn't reported as income, was to keep flowing until the house was paid off.

As the story goes, Bonds would sit and sign baseballs for hours to raise money for Bell. Although Bonds had millions, his accountants (and his wife) had control over (or at least access to) his finances. By appearing at card shows and signing baseballs, Bonds could earn cash that did not need to be disclosed to his accountants—cash his wife, Liz, would never know about. Before long, Bonds had managed to give Bell $80,000 in cash, which she used to make a down payment on a house in Scottsdale, Arizona. Bell promptly quit her job and moved into the new house. From there, it was all downhill. Bell couldn't find a job that would pay her enough to live on, but Bonds said he didn't have any more money for her.

Apparently, Bonds had a new groupie friend, a model he had met in New York. And that led to the third big mistake Bonds made in dealing with Bell. Bell says they had an argument in mid-2003. According to Bell, Bonds acted schizophrenic, one minute telling her he wanted her to move to Los Angeles where he was building a home, and the next calling her to say she needed "to disappear." When Bell inquired as to the duration of her contemplated disappearance, Bonds's response was sharp and bitter. "Did I f*ckin' stutter?" he asked rhetorically. Then he added, "Maybe forever."

Not surprisingly, Bell was angry. She let Bonds know that she knew about the New York model who was serving as her substitute groupie, asking, "Are you going to make your girlfriend in New York disappear, too?"

For Bonds this was a big swing and a miss—a definite strike three in his dealings with Bell. From that point forward, those who wanted to convince the world that Bonds had used steroids would have a tremendous ally in Bell.

By late 2003, as BALCO was being raided, Bell had decided to hire an attorney to try to force Bonds to pay for the rest of her house. As their respective attorneys negotiated, Bell's attorney emphasized that Bell had the bank records to show that Bonds had given her a lot of cash. In addition, Bonds's attorneys were told about those stupid voice-mail messages Bonds had left and about the fact that the tapes had been kept. And finally, Bell was willing to tell the world that Bonds had admitted to her that he was using "supplements." Not steroids—"supplements."

Bonds allegedly offered Bell $20,000 to shut up and go away. Bell wanted six figures. So there was no deal. Bell sold the house (likely netting a tidy profit), but she wanted more money and she wanted to get even with Bonds. When she heard that Congress was suddenly interested in baseball, Bell emailed Senator John McCain and provided him with the dirt on Bonds. With government spending generating unprecedented federal deficits, with Osama bin Laden still on the loose, and with large numbers of U.S. troops getting killed every month in Iraq, McCain somehow managed to stay busy enough to avoid responding to Bell's email.

So Bell did what any self-respecting ex-lover would do—she hooked up with the true-crime author and TV talk-show fixture Aphrodite Jones. Together, Jones and Bell finagled an *At Large with Geraldo Rivera* television appearance on February 12, 2005. The goal was to get a lucrative book deal.

The always clever Geraldo asked Bell if she had any evidence that Bonds used what Geraldo called "steeroids." Bell calmly explained that she was "familiar with…all of the changes that occurred in his body…as a result of the intimate relationship that we did have." Bell educated Geraldo, telling him that the physical changes that proved Bonds's steroid use "included everything from acne on his back to a great deal of bloating." Bell explained that she also observed so-called 'roid rage. Incongruously, Bell said that when Bonds got mad he would draw his hand back as if he was going to hit her. He did it "just to see me flinch so that he could laugh about it."

Jones jumped in and explained that Bell had been with Bonds from 1994 to 2003. According to Jones, Bonds's behavior didn't start to change until he allegedly admitted steroid use to Bell. Jones left viewers with the impression that it was Bonds's decision to *admit* steroid use that led to a behavioral change—not Bonds's actual use of steroids. Yes, for those who were watching, confusion was hard to avoid.

When pressed, Bell argued that Bonds had admitted using steroids between 1999 and 2000. Bell and Jones suggested Bonds had self-diagnosed an arm injury he suffered because steroids caused his muscles to grow too fast.

Eventually, Jones jumped back in to explain that this story was much bigger than steroids. Jones reminded Geraldo that Bonds had promised Bell a house. Jones explained, "She lived 10 years with this man. He said he would take care of her for the rest of his life. He owned her. He controlled her. That's his way; Bonds likes to control."

Then Geraldo asked Bell about her efforts to settle with Bonds privately. Bell explained that there was no settlement because "he offered me peanuts for the whole thing." Geraldo was ultimately prompted to ask: "Are you a gold digger, Kimberly?" Bell's answer: "Absolutely not."

Geraldo had his "exclusive" interview, and he concluded by plugging Bell's contemplated book, *Bonds Girl*.

Jeff Novitzky must be a big Geraldo fan (and really, who isn't?). Within a few days of Bell's appearance on Geraldo's show, Bell received a visit from the IRS agent. Novitzky was interested in steroids and the potential tax evasion implications that related to Bonds's desire to generate cash from card shows so he could give Bell money without his wife knowing about it.

Suddenly, it was Bell's turn to testify. Bell told stories about acne on Bonds's back, his balding (which was now also blamed on steroids), and his emotional outbursts. She was asked whether HGH had made his head swell. Bell thought it was possible.

Grand jurors even asked about Bonds's testicles. Unfortunately for Bonds, he had raised the ascending testicle issue a couple of weeks earlier while he was talking with reporters. Bonds had told reporters he had no physical symptoms of steroid use, noting that "I can tell you my testicles are the same size." Bonds said his testicles "haven't shrunk." Now, a grand juror was reading Bonds's words to Bell and asking for her opinion. (Hey, is this a great country, or what?) Bell believed Bonds's testicles had shrunk, at least a little.

Soon it was late 2007. Bonds was now baseball's Home Run King and Bell still didn't have her money. She still didn't have her book deal. But Bell would not be ignored. It was time to use the Margo Adams playbook. Bell made a splash of sorts in the November 2007 issue of *Playboy*. *Playboy* probably wasn't going to pay Bell a lot of money for merely repeating the information she had relayed on

Geraldo's show in 2005. And judging from the pictures, it probably wasn't going to pay her a lot of money to pose for photos without the benefit of substantial clothing. She had to come up with something new. So it came as no surprise that Bell was able to add a few new details to her story in late 2007. For starters, Bell told us Bonds had "choked" her in 2003 during their last meeting, a minor upgrade from her prior descriptions of Bonds placing a hand on her throat. And now Bell had better recall with respect to Bonds's testicle size. A few years earlier she said that although they hadn't disappeared, Bonds's testicles were not as big as they used to be. In 2007 she told *Playboy* his testicles had "shriveled up."

According to Bell, Bonds sometimes went behind closed doors with Greg Anderson. Although she didn't know what it contained, Bell noticed that Bonds took his little satchel with him. In a slight twist from what had previously been reported, Bell said Bonds told her he started using steroids to speed his recovery from an elbow injury, but he came to believe steroids had just made the injury worse. Despite that profound admission, the two never discussed steroids again.

The Secret Tape Recording

In 2003 a former athlete (who does not want his identity revealed) struck up a conversation with Bonds's trainer, Anderson. Anderson didn't know their conversation was being recorded. The person who made the clandestine, nine-minute, 19-second recording—or possibly someone else—apparently supplied a copy to the *Shadows* authors, Williams and Fainaru-Wada. They say Anderson's voice has been identified by two more anonymous people who know Anderson and listened to the tape.

In the parts of the secret recording the *Shadows* authors have been willing to quote, Anderson spends considerable time trying to convince his conversation partner that he really knows steroids.

During the discussion, Anderson reportedly addressed some of the problems steroid users face as follows, "What happens is, they put too much in one area, and what it does, it will actually ball up and puddle, and what happens is, it will eat away and make an indentation, and it's a cyst. It makes a big f*cking cyst, and you have to drain it. Oh, no, it's gnarly."

Anderson also is said to have bragged about his inside knowledge of baseball's steroid-testing program. We are told that on the undercover tape he claimed, "We know when they're going to do it," referring to "random" testing, and he bragged that he would know about it a week or two in advance.

Anderson also discussed a temporarily slumping Bonds on the tape. The *Shadows* authors explain that Anderson said on tape that Bonds "thinks the magic's gone, [that] he doesn't have it anymore." Playing the role of a sports psychologist, Anderson is said to have explained that "it's generated by his mind. He's afraid he's like losing it, but like I told him, he's way too nice. Talking to reporters, being way too nice—be an asshole again! Every time he is an asshole, it just f*cking works. He f*cking plays good because he's being himself."

Although the quoted parts of the secret tape do not actually have Anderson saying that Bonds used steroids, or even that Anderson gave him steroids, the *Shadows* authors say Anderson claimed, "Barry Bonds was using an 'undetectable' performance-enhancing drug during the 2003 baseball season."

Odds and Ends

Was there any other reason for people to believe Bonds took steroids, that he did so knowingly, and that the ingestion of steroids was the reason he was surpassing Babe Ruth and Hank Aaron? Yes!

Olympic shot-putter C.J. Hunter, once Marion Jones's husband, told Novitzky that Conte had told him Bonds was using the Clear.

Five other major league baseball players apparently told the grand jury that they got steroids, HGH, and other substances from Bonds's trainer, Anderson. In addition, some say Sheffield told the grand jury that Anderson gave him the Cream and the Clear and that he took those substances at Bonds's direction. In his recent book, *Inside Power*, Sheffield says Anderson gave him a cream to use on his knees after surgical stitches popped out during a set of squats. And, of course, Sheffield also says he checked with a doctor who said the cream "was not that different from the Neosporin you buy at Rite Aid."

Sprinter Tim Montgomery told the grand jury Conte had said he was giving Winstrol to Bonds.

Documents that were confiscated from Anderson's apartment included one that referenced "BLB 2003." ("BLB," of course, are Bonds's initials.) The document had notations that arguably referred to HGH, the Clear, the Cream, and insulin. Other documents "associated with Bonds" are thought to have referenced trenbolone and "beans"—the Mexican steroid that can be taken orally. Finally, some documents suggested that Bonds's blood had been sent for testing.

The strength of the case against Bonds is the subject of serious dispute. To the San Francisco Giants, the case was built on little more than innuendo and speculation. Rafael Palmeiro had tested positive for steroids—not Bonds. Canseco said he injected steroids into Mark McGwire—not Bonds.

However, many believe the fact that Bonds was chasing records their heroes set was itself proof of steroid use. As Hall of Famer Reggie Jackson explained, "Henry Aaron never hit 50 home runs in a season. So you're going to tell me that you're a greater hitter than Henry Aaron? Bonds hit 73, and he would have hit 100 if they would have pitched to him. I mean, come on, now. There is no way you can outperform Aaron and Ruth and Mays at that level."

Some disliked Bonds so intensely that the question of whether he used steroids was merely academic—they felt Bonds should be attacked no matter what. Christine Brennan's September 8, 2005, *USA Today* column spoke for many when she said, "How we wish we could just avoid Bonds once and for all, have him and those muscles, however they were made, fade away, never to return."

5

It Sure Looks Like He's on Steroids

Barry Bonds just looks like he's on steroids! As "proof" of Bonds's alleged steroid use, his accusers say Bonds:

1. Gained all that weight
2. Suddenly had muscles
3. Had acne on his back
4. Saw his head grow
5. Saw his hair fall out
6. Saw his testicles shrink

Is the way a person looks really evidence of anything? Does the way a person looks really prove anything?

Maybe—maybe in the broadest sense the way Bonds looks is at least arguably some evidence of steroid use. After all, the law uses a fairly generous definition of the word *evidence*. When attorneys and judges use the word *evidence*, they are not always using it the way a scientist would. If a scientist wants to figure out if a person is on steroids, the scientist subjects the person's blood or urine to a battery of tests. A scientist would be reluctant to just look at a Ben Johnson or Floyd Landis and proclaim, "Yeah, he is taking the juice." From a scientific standpoint, the way Bonds looks isn't reliable evidence of steroid use.

So let's pretend to be scientists for a minute. As far as we know, Bonds has never tested positive for steroids. (If you remember hearing about a positive test for amphetamines, you have a good memory for rumors. But amphetamines aren't steroids and they don't build muscle.) So the kind of evidence that would normally be required to ruin a person's reputation isn't readily available. It just doesn't exist. But less compelling evidentiary substitutes do exist. People who claim the way Bonds looks is evidence of his steroid use are using a cheap substitute for real evidence.

In the court of public opinion, and even in the legal courts, scientific evidence isn't required. If it exists, it's a bonus. A California jurist will tell you that evidence is just about anything that can be "presented to the senses" and tends to support the "existence or nonexistence" of a particular fact. This doesn't mean it's entirely a free-for-all in court. Evidence still has to be considered legally relevant. And much of what might qualify as relevant evidence still does not qualify as admissible evidence—evidence that is allowed to impact the result of a litigated case. Let's take an example. Someone could argue that the fact that Bonds was involved in a messy divorce might indicate "'roid rage" and constitute evidence of steroid use. But even if we were charitable enough to treat the messy divorce as relevant to "'roid rage" or steroid use, it wouldn't rise to the level of *admissible* evidence. Whatever steroid relevancy the divorce might have is far outweighed by the real purpose for making the argument—to remind us that Bonds is a bad guy. So even in court, not everything goes. Judges filter a lot of "evidence" so that it never gets to the jury. But the standard is loose.

Other types of evidence that are not generally allowed in court, even if they might become prominent in the court of public opinion, include privileged discussions between an attorney and client and hearsay. Although there are exceptions, in court, "hearsay" is typically excluded, so that person A usually isn't allowed to say that person B told person A that a particular fact was true. Likewise, communications between a client and the client's attorney are usually not admissible in evidence—at least not when the client wants confidentiality. The law makes such discussions privileged based on the assumption that society will be better off if people are free to converse with their attorneys without worrying about the possibility that a jury might ultimately be invited to scrutinize their dialogue.

Anyway, if Bonds was on trial for robbing a liquor store would we let people "prove" he robbed the liquor store just by saying that he looks like a robber? Of course not! We would want an eyewitness to say, "I know Barry Bonds. I was in the liquor store that day. I saw Bonds walk in carrying a large baseball bat. I heard Bonds yell at the clerk, 'Hey, do you know who I am? I'm the home-run king. Now give me all the money in the register, or I'll use this bat to turn your brains into mush.'" That's direct evidence—the kind of evidence José Canseco is willing to offer about Mark McGwire and several other players. Canseco says he personally injected McGwire and Rafael Palmeiro with steroids. But no one says he or she injected Bonds with steroids. Unable to amass any direct evidence, and lacking scientific evidence, we're stuck looking at things like, well, the way Bonds looks.

*

There is a problem with the "Bonds gained all that weight overnight, so he must have used steroids" argument. The problem is that the statement is not supported by evidence. The argument that Bonds must have been on steroids because he suddenly gained a lot of weight is usually presented in an exaggerated misleading way.

In 2005, Canseco published his book, *Juiced*. Between meandering stories about driving too fast, marital discord, how baseball players handle cell phones in a way that lets them quickly distinguish between wives and groupies, and visits to Madonna "Like a Virgin" Louise

Veronica Ciccone's apartment, *Juiced* provides us with a bit of insight as to how Canseco allegedly introduced some of his teammates to steroids.

Bonds and Canseco were never teammates. Nevertheless, Canseco's version of the "Bonds must have been on steroids" argument goes something like this. Early in 2000 Bonds and Canseco participated in a home-run-hitting contest at Cashman Field in Las Vegas. When Bonds saw Canseco, "he just stood there and stared." The always ultramodest Canseco says, "I weighed about 255 at that point, and I was just shredded with veins. Barry couldn't believe what he was seeing." According to Canseco, Bonds asked him, "What the hell have you been doing?" Bonds asked the question slowly and dramatically, so everyone would be sure to hear. Canseco points out that he won the contest, hitting some shots that went around 600 feet and landed on Washington Avenue. Canseco believes his stellar performance made a big impression on Bonds.

Canseco never says he told Bonds about steroids. He doesn't say he gave Bonds steroids. He doesn't even say he worked out with Bonds. And he certainly doesn't say he injected Bonds with steroids. What Canseco does say is this: "So what did Barry Bonds do that next off-season? He showed up in spring 2001 with 40 pounds of added muscle. As soon as he set foot on the field in Scottsdale that spring, he was all anyone could talk about. 'My God, look how big he is,' everyone was saying. 'He's monstrous. Look at him.'"

To be nice about it, we can say Canseco was exaggerating. But if we wanted to be accurate, we might just say Canseco was wrong or even making things up. Bonds may have added 15 pounds but did not add anything close to 40 pounds in a single off-season.

A certain amount of weight gain in men—especially married men—is probably to be expected between the ages of 20 and 40. We might typically think of it as "filling out." For a person who is over 6' tall, a gain of 15 or 20 pounds over a 20-year period wouldn't be the least bit surprising or unusual. And it might not even be noticeable. This would be true even if the individual gaining weight made no concerted effort to lift weights, build muscle, and win baseball games.

Barry's father, Bobby, pretty much invented the idea of a leadoff hitter who could hit a lot of home runs and steal a lot of bases. Bobby hit a lot of home runs—332. But he stole far more bases—461. Between 1969 and 1978, Bobby stole more than 40 bases in a season seven times. He was fast. He had power, but he had more speed.

When Barry Bonds joined the Pirates in 1986, they put him at the top of the order as the leadoff hitter. Like father, like son. Sure, Barry had some power. But he still had a speedster's build, weighing in at "only" 185 or 190 pounds. During his first four years in the majors, Bonds hit leadoff. He hit 84 home runs—an average of 21 per season—during those first four years. In contrast, during his first four years Bonds stole 117 bases—an average of just under 30 a season.

But then Bonds was moved to the middle of the batting order, and power became a priority. To be sure, he still had speed. But his power and his physique were starting to develop more noticeably. Even before Brady Anderson hit 50 home runs in 1996, and long before Bonds was accused of using steroids (which allegedly started after the 1998 season, at the earliest), Bonds had started the workout and weight-lifting regimen that would ultimately remodel his body.

In the off-season between 1992 and 1993, Bonds started working out under the supervision of Jim Warren, a personal trainer who usually worked with football players. According to Warren, "Our goal was for [Bonds] to become a 50-home run, 50-steal player." Warren explains:

> We did a ton of sprinting and weights. [Bonds] was as thin
> as a whippet when I started working with him. But by the
> time he reported, he was an athletic freak—Terrell Owens
> with a baseball bat. We're talking about a 4.4 sprinter who
> can dunk a basketball, shoot bows and arrows, and throw
> with either hand.

In *Love Me, Hate Me*, Jeff Pearlman had this to say about Bonds reporting to spring training in 1993: "Unlike veteran first baseman [Will] Clark, who, as usual, reported to camp with the body of a soggy pear, Bonds sported a newly barreled chest, oak-tree arms, powerful legs, and 8 percent body fat."

So, long before 2001, Bonds no longer had the build of a whippet. Although he still had speed, he was gaining weight, gaining muscle, and getting bigger. This was early in 1993, more than five years before anyone accuses Bonds of having taken steroids and seven years before Canseco falsely says Bonds suddenly grew muscles and gained 40 pounds all at once.

By the mid-1990s, any idea that lifting weights might retard a player's swing and hurt his performance was becoming antiquated. By 1996, Bonds was bench-pressing 315 pounds (up from 230), hitting the ball harder than ever, and looking more and more like a football player in a baseball uniform. And this was still years before anyone says he may have started taking steroids.

The *Shadows* authors do little to hide their bias. Their book's first page of photos is telling. The page has three photos: a picture of Bonds in 1983 as a college freshman; a picture of Bonds "as a young Pittsburgh Pirate" (where he is described as "long and lean, with a build like a marathoner"), and a picture of Bonds in 2005—a full two decades later—grimacing as he flexes and places pressure on a batting helmet to pump up his chest and arms for the camera. Williams and

Fainaru-Wada described the last picture like this: "After BALCO, Bonds, shown here at SBC Park in September 2005, resembled an NFL linebacker."

But they were willing to defend McGwire. The *Shadows* authors noted that although McGwire had "bulked up," he was already "a big man" when he hit 49 home runs as a rookie in 1987. In contrast, they describe Bonds as having "morphed over the years." They say Bonds looked like a "WWE wrestler" or a "toy superhuman action figure."

Comparing a Bonds 1987 photo to a Bonds 2001 or 2005 photo is misleading. It is misleading because it does not address the 14 to 18 years between the two photos. And by the way, how many of us still look like we did when we were first-year college students?

The argument that Bonds started taking steroids in 1998, as *Shadows* contends, or in 2000, as Canseco contends, and suddenly gained 40 pounds is not true. A March 8, 1998, article in *The Atlanta Journal-Constitution* reveals one of the major flaws in the argument. The article says Bonds reported to 1998 spring training in what he described as his "best shape in years." Bonds had actually lost 8 pounds, reducing his weight from 220 to 212. So, even if Bonds ultimately made it up to 228 (or maybe even a few pounds more), he did not come close to suddenly gaining 40 pounds. Bonds gained weight because he was getting older and working out. His weight gain was progressive over the years and not a one-time, sudden event. The bulk of his weight gain occurred *before* anyone says he might have started using steroids.

Think about it—*before* Bonds ever purportedly took a single dose of any steroid, he had matured and already weighed between 210 to 220 pounds. He had already improved his bench press capability by a whopping 35 percent. Those who contend Bonds must have been on steroids because he suddenly gained 40 pounds are relying on falsehoods. It's as simple as that.

*

What about all the muscles? Isn't that evidence of steroid use?

Angelo Siciliano never took a steroid. He was at the beach one day when a stranger walked by and literally kicked sand in his face. Siciliano did not react, but his girlfriend did. She got up and walked away, and Siciliano never saw her again. Siciliano was thin. He figured the unfortunate incident was the direct result of a lack of muscle. The incident ate at him and ate at him. Finally, he decided he had had enough. It was time to pack on some muscle.

Did Siciliano turn to steroids? No! During a visit to the zoo, Siciliano noticed how lions and tigers flexed their muscles against the bars of their cages, using resistance to train their muscles. Suddenly, Siciliano had an idea—an idea that would change his life. He developed a workout methodology called dynamic tension. Siciliano used dynamic tension to develop enormous biceps and a powerful, if not hulking, physique. Without the aid of steroids, Siciliano became so well muscled that he decided to compete in bodybuilding competitions, including a New York competition that was searching for "the world's most perfectly developed man."

Siciliano's dedication had been so great, his body had become so incredibly different from what it used to be, that he actually won the contest. And he did it without using a single steroid. Now, if Siciliano's story has a familiar ring, it's because Siciliano later changed his name to Charles Atlas. Siciliano won that bodybuilding contest in 1921, before steroids were invented. He went on to use the embarrassing but subsequently inspirational incident with the bully at the beach to found a thriving business that was based on his enormous arms and the idea that all of the world's "97-pound weaklings" could develop substantial muscles. Just because a person has big muscles doesn't mean the person used steroids.

Nevertheless, those who are determined to believe Bonds used steroids will point out that Bonds was in his mid-30s when he was developing his muscles. Again, the argument takes liberties. Bonds was 28 in 1993, when he really started developing muscle—not in his mid-30s. But even if we allow the Bonds antagonists to make up the facts, we might still decide that their argument proves nothing.

If you really believe that a man in his mid-30s or older cannot develop and maintain a powerful physique, please allow me to introduce you to Jack LaLanne.

LaLanne was born in 1914. LaLanne's father was overweight, and he died of a heart attack at age 50. Improbably, LaLanne was a skinny boy who was addicted to sugar. He would eat ice cream until it made him sick. His diet was so poor, people blamed it for his mental problems. Maybe that was an exaggeration, but he did assault his own brother, attempt suicide, and try to burn the family house down.

One day LaLanne attended a Paul Bragg lecture at the Oakland Women's City Club. Bragg had founded the nation's first health-food store in the 1920s. During the lecture, he looked at LaLanne and told the audience, "It matters not what your age is or your physical condition; if you obey nature's laws, you can be born again." Bragg explained the healthy life meant that white sugar, white flour, red meat, and processed foods should be avoided.

That one lecture changed LaLanne's life. He started eating right and taking vitamins—and he started lifting weights. Soon, LaLanne was captain of his football team. Although he'd been planning a possible career in medicine, he dropped out of college to open the nation's first gym, using money he won in bodybuilding competitions and earned by serving as a personal trainer for police officers and firefighters.

Through exercise and clean living, LaLanne developed incredible muscle that he displayed on national TV when he did 1,000 push-ups in less than 20 minutes. By the late 1950s, he had his own national television show. The show ran for 34 years, with the muscular LaLanne teaching viewers the benefits of physical fitness. This is the man who invented the jumping jack.

Some professional athletes sought LaLanne's assistance. But, according to LaLanne, coaches usually forbade such training, fearing that their players would become overly muscle-bound. But LaLanne never stopped his own workout routine. As an octogenarian, he still donned his trademark jumpsuit, with the sleeves cut high to better display his powerful arms. For many years LaLanne is said to have looked "like two equilateral triangles joined at one corner."

No doubt, LaLanne was a bit extreme. He says his father died because he gorged himself on "cheese and other poisons." Nevertheless, with a healthy lifestyle and limitless appetite for exercise as guiding principles, LaLanne demonstrated that men could be in tremendous physical shape in their 30s, or their 40s, or 50s, 60s, 70s, or beyond.

LaLanne liked to celebrate his major birthdays in style. When he turned 40, he swam the Golden Gate Channel. Not a big deal, except he was towing a 2,000-pound cabin cruiser. For his 60th birthday he swam from Alcatraz to Fishermen's Wharf. This time, the boat he was towing weighed a little less—but his wrists were handcuffed together. When he turned 70, LaLanne swam part of the Long Beach Harbor. He did it while pulling 70 boats.

LaLanne was passionate about fitness. He was quoted as saying:

> If you have a six-inch tool and a 50-inch waistline, the thing doesn't look very big, does it? When you married a beautiful girl and all of a sudden you start seeing her tits down to here and her breath stinks and she's not clean anymore and has no pride in herself, you can't love her. You may bullshit yourself, but you can't. Energy makes people beautiful. That's what charisma is. You don't want to be close to someone who's dead and crapped out all the time, who's bitching that it's a lousy f*cking world and "Christ, my

ulcers are killing me." Maybe 50 or 60 percent of all divorces
are predicated on someone's being physically unfit.

LaLanne explained that there's no one set rule for aging or
physical fitness. It may be true that "the average person who is 70
or 80 is over the hill." According to LaLanne, "They're fat, they're
racked with aches and pains." But, he adds, "Then you get people
over 90 who are running marathons because they worked at living. I
have a lot of energy, and you know why? Because I use it. It's use it or
lose it, and it's believing in something."

Barry Bonds believed he was baseball's most talented player ever.
He used his talent, and he believed weight training could help him
build muscle and become an even better hitter. Does that mean he
used steroids? Well, did Jack LaLanne use steroids?

Countless people have managed to add large quantities of muscle
to their bodies. And they did it without steroids. Organizations such
as the World Natural Bodybuilding Federation—an organization
comprised of people who make Bonds look like a softy—offer a
weight-lifting culture that is absent steroids.

Although Bonds has the advantage of significant wealth and a
lengthy off-season—two factors that help give him the time to engage
in rigorous weight training—many steroid-free bodybuilders have
managed to pack on lots of muscle while working regular jobs to
support themselves. Unlike Bonds, these committed amateurs can't
afford multiple personal trainers or assistants to take care of things
such as shopping, dry cleaning, banking, or cleaning the house. They
can't afford a personal chef. Still, they are living, breathing proof that
it is possible to build significant amounts of muscle without ever
taking steroids.

Take Darin Steen, for example. Steen is "ripped," with enormous muscles sprouting from his arms, chest, and legs. Even though he's in his 40s, he is enormous. Steen worked as a truck driver for 18 years until he finally decided to become a personal trainer on a full-time basis. He regularly participates in competitive bodybuilding contests that screen and test the athletes to ensure that no one is using steroids. After years of hard work and dedication, Steen is now considered a professional, steroid-free bodybuilder. Steen explains his approach:

> To me, functional training is doing explosive-type plyometrics and power movements. For the most part, it is also staying off of machines that do all the balancing and stabilizing for you. Usually it's done with free weights or just body weight (plus added weights, vests, or belts). I incorporate at least one functional movement per workout per body part. In a perfect world, I would periodize and do functional movements and no traditional bodybuilding-type movements for a couple months a year—possibly get involved in rock climbing, track and field, rowing, etc. Some of the best physiques I had ever seen do this. Psychologically it is very difficult, especially at first.

Steen engages in grueling workouts, pushing the weights to the point of absolute exhaustion. When he's training, it is six days a week. He focuses on his chest on Mondays, arms on Tuesdays, hamstrings on Wednesdays, back on Thursdays, shoulders on Fridays, and legs on Saturdays.

How old is too old? The Bonds bashers say you can't build substantial muscle after age 30. Is that true? When does a man who dedicates himself to intense weight training stop seeing results? Is it true that a Barry Bonds in his mid-30s couldn't have experienced significant muscle gains without taking steroids? Not according to

Steen. Steen says that because "drug-free for life competitive body-building is, for the most part, slow going, I believe most competitors should peak around the age of 46 or 47." Steen goes on to note that people who go for the "quick fix"—steroids—peak sooner and have shorter careers.

Steen's view reminds us of the way McGwire, Canseco, Sammy Sosa, and a few other players broke down physically. Their skills and abilities evaporated almost instantaneously. When he was 37 years old, McGwire could only hit .187. He struck out 118 times in 2001 and walked only 56 times. He was terrible.

After turning 30, Canseco never came close to being the player that he was in his 20s. There was only one post-30 season in which Canseco had 100 RBIs. In 1998 (when he was 33) he hit 46 home runs and drove in 107. He also managed to steal 29 bases. But even that year, Canseco's batting average was only .237. He struck out 159 times and walked only 65 times. He was caught stealing 17 times. Canseco played three more seasons, with his power figures rapidly dropping, a batting average nowhere near .300, and base stealing no longer a part of his game. He was out of the league after 2001. He was 36 years old.

Between 1998 and 2002, Sosa had five incredible power years. He hit 66, 63, 50, 64, and 49 home runs—an average of 58.4 per year. Sosa was only 29 years old in 1998 and 33 in 2002. Sosa had decent years when he was 34 and 35. He still managed to hit 40 and 35 home runs in those years. But his skills were already eroding noticeably. In 2003 Sosa struck out 143 times and walked only 62 times. By 2004 a 35-year-old Sosa could hit only .253, and he struck out 133 times while walking only 56 times. By 2005 there was nothing left in Sosa's tank. As a 36-year-old, Sosa could manage only 14 home runs while batting .221. He didn't play in 2006, and he was only a little better when he came back to play for the Texas Rangers in 2007.

Other suspected steroid users fit the same pattern. The Houston Astros' Jeff Bagwell was an MVP as a 26-year-old in 1994, when he hit

39 home runs in 400 at-bats. At age 33 in 2001, Bagwell hit 39 home runs, with 43 doubles. He stole 11 bases and drove in 130 runs. At age 36, however, Bagwell's numbers declined noticeably. And as a 37-year-old, he hit only three home runs. His career was over. There is no proof that Bagwell ever used steroids. But his sudden physical collapse might make someone wonder.

When he was 33 years old, Ken Caminiti won the National League MVP, and we know he was on steroids. He admitted it openly. It was 1996, and Caminiti hit .326, belted 40 home runs, and drove in 130 runs. Within a few years, Caminiti was injured so often he couldn't play half a season. In 2001, when he was 38, he played a little more often, but he was no longer productive. His average had dropped to .228. He struck out 85 times and walked only 43 times. He had only 15 home runs. His career was over. And unfortunately, he died in 2004.

Perhaps Steen is on to something: maybe an athlete who uses steroids is particularly likely to break down and fall apart. If so, Bonds does not fit the steroid-user profile. After having a monstrous year in 2001 (when he hit 73 home runs), Bonds had three more solid years at ages 37, 38, and 39. In each of those seasons—playing at an age when other suspected steroid users had demonstrated a sharp decline in abilities or had already retired—Bonds never hit fewer than 45 home runs. His *lowest* batting average in those three seasons was .341. Bonds's *highest* strikeout total was 58. He walked 198 times in 2002, as a 37-year-old. The 39-year-old Bonds drew an amazing 232 walks. Babe Ruth never walked more than 170 times in any one season.

In 2005 Bonds suffered a series of physical setbacks. Injuries to his knee kept him out of action almost the entire season. A yearlong layoff would be enough to erode the skills of a 27-year-old. But the 41-year-old Bonds returned in 2006 and had a respectable season. He hit 26 home runs in 367 at-bats, batted .270, and still managed to draw 115 walks, while striking out only 51 times. This is not consistent with a pattern of steroid use. If Bonds had been a heavy steroid user, we would have expected to see serious physical degradation several years ago. We would have expected markedly less productive statistics throughout his late 30s and particularly after a 2005 season in which Bonds participated in only 14 games. Then, in 2007, after turning 43 in July, Bonds was still the most potent offensive player on his team. Despite the stresses associated with the steroid hysteria and his relentless assault on Aaron's all-time home-run record, he continued to hit home runs and draw walks.

Muscles are not proof of steroid use. Just ask Kathy Roberts. Roberts is a lifetime, steroid-free, nationally recognized power lifter. She can bench press 265 pounds. She does 350-pound squats. She dead lifts 430 pounds. Roberts has a strong, powerful build. She got into power lifting to gain weight. And it has worked. She has competed in the 165-pound and 198-pound divisions, and she has outperformed many athletes who have been associated with steroid use. All that power, all that strength—and she has never used a steroid. When asked what she would change about her sport if she could, Roberts said:

> It would be to eliminate the drug use, the deceit, and the manipulation. I would also like to get rid of the total unfairness in the sport to genuine and naturally gifted athletes who tend to be overshadowed by drug use in many federations and magazines. I believe that in the long run that will come to a screeching halt as long as people stand firm to the truth and don't give in to what may be the majority.

Men and women who are willing to dedicate significant time and energy to weight training will gain muscle mass. Steroids are not an essential part of the formula.

Bodybuilders and power lifters are not the only ones who do amazing things to their bodies without using steroids. Julio Franco is just a baseball player, but he's proven that dedication can translate into good health and a superior physique beyond the mid-30s, beyond the late 30s, beyond the early 40s, beyond the mid-40s, and into the late 40s. Franco first played in the major leagues in 1982. He was 23 years old. As a young major league ballplayer, Franco was a drinker who liked to party into the early morning hours. After hitting .341 to win an American League batting title for Texas in 1991, Franco found religion and changed his ways. He started to eat better and sleep more. Alcohol was no longer part of his diet. But weight training was now part of his life.

Early in his career, Franco was listed at 6'0", and he weighed 155 pounds when he played for the Philadelphia Phillies in 1982. But over time, people change. Now, he is listed as an inch taller and 50 pounds heavier. The extra weight is muscle, not fat. Franco hit .273 for the New York Mets in 2006. He was "only" 47 years old. Franco's 47-year-old physique outshines those of teammates who are half his age. The muscular Franco wants to play until he's 50. His current contract will expire after his 49th birthday. No one wants to put Franco on trial for using steroids, but some people think he eats too many egg whites.

*

There is room to argue about the best player in the history of baseball. Ted Williams was awfully good, and he missed five years due to wartime military service. And what about Rogers Hornsby? He was dedicated. To preserve his eyesight, he refused to watch movies or read newspapers (although he occasionally peeked, but just to check on his batting average). Back in 1915—long before there were steroids—Hornsby hit .246. He wanted to do better. So he spent the winter doing demanding labor on his uncle's farm. He arrived for spring training in 1916 with an extra 30 pounds of muscle.

A Hall of Famer, Hornsby played most of his 23 seasons at second base. He hit 301 home runs and ended his career with a lifetime .358 batting average. Between 1921 and 1925, Hornsby hit .397, .401, .384, .424, and .403.

Everybody knows Babe Ruth could hit, but he actually started his career as a very good pitcher. In 1915 Ruth was 18–8, with a 2.44 earned-run average. In 1916 and 1917 Ruth won 23 and 24 games, respectively. His combined earned-run average over the course of those seasons was less than 2.00. At 714 home runs, with a lifetime .342 batting average, you can argue that Ruth was a better all-around player than Bonds. But it's just an argument. After all, Ruth played in a segregated league, where many of the top players were not allowed to compete because of their skin color.

But one thing we can't really argue about is this: no baseball player has ever been more dedicated than Bonds. Not Williams, Hornsby, Ty Cobb, Nolan Ryan, or Joe DiMaggio. Bonds is dedicated and committed, and he is extremely focused. When Bonds devoted his energy to weight training, the results were spectacular. He may not have been the equal of Steen or even Roberts, but Bonds's dedication means, at the very least, that his muscularity cannot be considered proof of steroid use.

To be sure, Bonds used creatine, protein supplements, and amino acids. But these aren't steroids: they are natural substances and perfectly legal. Bonds was concerned about his health, and he was willing to sacrifice by taking a pass on life's little pleasures. Unlike his father, Bonds was not a drinker. And since many of his teammates didn't particularly like Barry, social commitments didn't keep him from working out.

In *Ball Four* Jim Bouton describes a typical night out. Bouton says he "remembered doing a strip to my underwear to the theme song of *Lawrence of Arabia* and then treading water in the swimming pool with a martini in each hand and *then* going out and beating the Angels the next night." If you remember *Ball Four* you know Bouton describes a lot more than that.

Bouton was pitching (and partying) in the 1960s. He won 21 games in 1963 and 18 games in 1964. The rest of his career was nothing to write home about. So, unlike most professional baseball players, Bouton is best known for writing a book. In 1970, *Ball Four* introduced the public to the fact that many major leaguers are not exactly the world's most dedicated athletes. Today's players don't smoke cigarettes in the dugout. But, like Ruth before them, even today, many players cannot resist the temptation to drink heavily and chase women, often late into the night.

That was *never* Bonds. Instead, Bonds could often be found at the ballpark, doing yoga, running, and lifting weights—all before 8:00 in the morning. As his teammate Stan Javier put it, Bonds would "be in the weight room before the game, be in the weight room after the game, be in the weight room all the time, day after day."

Particularly with Greg Anderson as his trainer, Bonds's workouts were grueling. He describes sessions involving up to 16 sets of repetitions for various muscles. A typical five-day rotation might involve up to 14 sets per day, with 10 repetitions per set of exercises as varied as Hammer-machine presses, barbell squats, cable triceps press-downs, dead lifts, and low-back extensions. Bonds tried to do each set at the maximum bearable weight.

After the 2001 season—after Bonds had already established a new single-season home-run record by hitting 73 of them—Gary Sheffield visited him. In fact, Sheffield lived with Bonds for two months. Bonds made sure Sheffield was awake every morning by 6:00 AM.

Each morning started with a running and cardiovascular workout. Then they were off to Pac Bell Park for batting practice. After batting practice, they went to Burlingame for intense weight training with Greg Anderson at World Gym.

The regimen was too much for Sheffield, who had befriended Bonds after hitting 36 home runs for the Dodgers in 2001 (perhaps because Sheffield hoped training with Bonds might result in better numbers and an even bigger contract). But Bonds's nearly psychotic dedication quickly wore Sheffield out. And the two proved that it is very hard for roommates to get along, even when both are multimillionaires. An argument, apparently over a rental car, ended the experiment. And Bonds's intensity (coupled with an inability to motivate without belittling) probably ended the friendship.

No one has ever been more committed to being the world's best baseball player than Bonds. If weight training can produce muscle without steroid ingestion (and we know it can), then Bonds's physique is not proof of steroid use.

Eating banana splits is a great way to gain weight. But, if you see a heavy person, you do not have proof that that heavy person eats a lot of banana splits. In fact, the heavy person may not even eat bananas. Assuming every heavy person eats too many banana splits (or eats any banana splits) is really nothing more than stereotyping. It just isn't proof of anything. And that same logic works for muscles and steroids. There may be a connection, but there may not be.

Before we leave the "Bonds suddenly sprouted muscles" argument, we need to think about one more thing. Mark Silva is a certified orthotist. That's not a bird watcher, it's someone who makes devices that assist or protect the body. Silva's most prominent work is the protective elbow device Bonds has been wearing for more than a decade. Bonds's elbow device is custom made. In the early years, a mold was made from Bonds's arm and used to custom fit the device. Then Silva started using precision calipers to measure Bonds's arm.

If there was no change in Bonds's arm size, there was no need to re-invent the wheel by making new (expensive and time-consuming molds) of Bonds's arm. Get ready for this— there was no change in Bonds's arm size after 1995. That's right, Silva says he hasn't had to re-mold Bonds's arm since 1995, and that's at least three years before Bonds allegedly started using steroids.

But what about Barry Bonds's alleged back acne? His baldness? The fact that his testicles are said to have shrunk, at least ever so slightly? And what about the fact that some people say Bonds's head has actually grown to the point where he resembles a human bobble-head doll? Is any of this proof that Bonds uses steroids?

The *Shadows* authors (with the help of Kimberly Bell, who had told Geraldo about the acne on Bonds's back) say that "Bonds's back broke out in acne, and he would stand in front of the bathroom mirror and say, 'Oh my God, I don't know where this is coming from.'" It is said that back acne is a Winstrol side effect.

Do we have scores of detailed scientific medical studies that prove the causal connection between acne (or other perceived side effects) and steroids? Not exactly. Medical professionals really aren't in a good position to do controlled studies of what happens when people take anabolic steroids in large doses. A Canadian medical professor who has served as a physician at five Olympic games, Dr. Andrew Pipe, explains, "We have no clinical experience with a clearly defined population of individuals taking clearly defined doses of anabolic steroids who have been followed for years to allow us to say with any degree of credibility exactly what the side effects might be." What would we think of doctors who gave people substances that are thought to cause prostate cancer and liver damage just to see if they get back acne? Dr. Warren

Willey summarizes the steroid hype problem by noting that "when someone delves into anabolic steroid use, unless they are stupid, they generally train harder, sleep more, and . . . eat better." And that leads to the problem of the various confounding factors. Most people who take large doses of anabolic steroids engage in certain associated behaviors, such as lifting weights. When we see changes in a steroid user's body, how can we be sure the steroids—rather than the associated behaviors—are responsible for the changes? The science that links steroids to acne may not be quite as strong as we thought it was.

Some people who take steroids do get acne. The speculation is that the extra testosterone that generates the androgenic, masculinizing impact of certain anabolic steroids can increase sebaceous gland activity. This might increase oil production in the skin, which inevitably leads to an oil crisis because all that oil can inflame the pores. Since the back has a lot of oil glands, people might get back acne when they take certain steroids.

There is a difference, however, between this type of educated guess, on the one hand, and evidence or proof, on the other. After all, it is no secret that sweat is a likely cause of back acne. It can stick to the clothes and skin. A sweaty back can cause the skin inflammation that results in acne.

Serious weight lifters sweat—whether they take steroids or not. A person who spends several hours a day engaged in intense weight training is going to sweat. It is also likely that many weight lifters are somewhat neglectful when it comes to cleaning the back. It is relatively easy to clean other parts of the body, but the back is hard to reach, particularly for someone who is sore from a hard workout. It seems likely that in the post-workout shower, the athlete may do a good job of cleaning the face, chest, arms, and legs. But even with a good scrub brush with a long handle, it can take patience and concentration to properly clean the back.

While there are people who want to associate Bonds's alleged back acne with steroid use, it seems more likely (or at least just as likely) that back acne results from sweat-producing workouts and the difficulty associated with properly cleaning the back. If sweat and cleansing (or lack thereof) were not the real cause of weight-lifter back acne, we would expect to see the acne manifest more uniformly in multiple locations on the skin. There is, after all, no reason for steroids to discriminate. The back may have a lot of oil glands, but it doesn't have a monopoly. If steroids are going to cause acne, why would it be limited to the back?

We haven't seen photographs of Bonds's pristine back in 1996 (he may have been lifting weights in 1996, but he certainly wasn't using steroids). For that matter, we don't have photographs of Bonds with an acne-laden back in 1999 or 2000 (when was allegedly using steroids). But even if we treat secondhand observations as entirely accurate, and even if we assume for the sake of argument that Bonds had the world's most severe case of back acne, we still can't say that it's proof that Bonds used steroids. The science to back up that contention just doesn't exist. Any case of back acne Bonds experienced may just as easily have been the result of intense workouts that created large quantities of sweat that could clog or inflame pores. Given that the back is one of the more difficult body areas to properly clean, a little back acne wouldn't be surprising even if Bonds never touched a steroid.

*

Steroids reduce the body's natural production of gonadotropins and certain hormones. As a result, many believe prolonged steroid use can cause testicular atrophy (or shrinkage) and reduced sperm counts. Ironically, steroid use is also blamed for increasing sex drive. Supposed evidence of these side effects has also been used to impeach Bonds. The *Shadows* authors tell us Bonds suffered from "sexual dysfunction." According to the book, Bell told a grand jury that although Bonds's testicles hadn't "disappeared," they were no longer "as big as they used to be."

Is this double dose of rumor and accusation evidence of steroid use? Well, if this is evidence, it isn't good evidence. Calling it flimsy would give it too much credit. First, getting a handle on the supposed side effects of steroids is extremely difficult. Controlled studies that effectively eliminate other variables and carefully quantify testicular atrophy among steroid users are few and far between. Maybe researchers are finding better things to do with their time.

Still, unsubstantiated argument raises other questions that are hard to avoid. How, for example, is testicle size measured? Do temperature variations affect the size? Are there different sizes at different times of day? Would size vary depending on time between the measurement and the test subject's most recent sexual activity?

And what about sexual dysfunction? At first it wasn't clear whether accusations of sexual dysfunction were aimed at infertility (which is often considered a possible steroid side effect) or erectile dysfunction. In her *Playboy* interview, Bell clarified—there were a few isolated occasions where Bonds couldn't perform. If steroids cause such a shortcoming, and if Bonds was regularly taking steroids, why would there only be a handful of erectile melt-downs? Could Bonds's sporadic inability to perform sexually for Bell have been caused by something other than steroids? Of course. Bonds was married, and he did have another girlfriend while he was seeing Bell. Maybe he was performing a little too often with other people. Maybe he was stressed, distracted, or worried about something else when he wasn't able to achieve and maintain tumescence. Maybe he had a few drinks that night. You get the point—there are many possible explanations for the occasional failed erection. And it can happen to men who never used steroids.

Bell didn't carefully measure Bonds's testicles, so she could not offer precise testimony. Could she be saying whatever it takes to make Bonds look bad? If Bonds was getting his advice from very knowledgeable steroid gurus, why wouldn't he be taking Human Chorionic Gonadotropin (HCG), the glycoprotein that prevents or reverses testicular atrophy?

To put it mildly, the offer of proof based on alleged shrinkage of Bonds's testicles, and the curious accusation of sexual dysfunction, are hard to follow. These contentions are too vague to be meaningful. How much shrinkage are we talking about? What kind and degree of sexual dysfunction are we talking about? From an objective viewpoint, these accusations really just don't add up to a hill of beans. But, from the standpoint of the accusers, they are almost perfect accusations. If someone already wants to believe Bonds hit home runs because he used steroids, all they have to do is conclude that Bonds's girlfriend confirms that Bonds's testicles shrank and that Bonds was having some unidentified sexual problem. So how could he not be using steroids?

Fortunately (or unfortunately, depending on who you are), we cannot go to the Internet and find photos of Bonds's allegedly shrinking testicles. There are no videos depicting Bonds's unsuccessful quest for proper sexual function. Instead, all we have to go on are vague accusations from a jilted lover who was well aware of the fact that no one is really in a position to disprove her claims.

But it gets worse. Even if we were absolutely certain that Bonds experienced testicular shrinkage and sexual dysfunction in any form, we would not have proof of anything. To one degree or another, low sperm counts, difficulty achieving or maintaining erection, and shrinking of the testicles are all associated with normal, everyday aging. Bonds was born in 1964. He is no spring chicken. So even if Ms. Bell really managed to observe (or even measure) some degree of testicular shrinkage or sexual dysfunction, it would not necessarily support the conclusion that the shrinkage or dysfunction was a result of steroid use.

*

It was a night to remember—May 19, 1994. The Seattle Mariners were playing the Texas Rangers. It was the first ever "Jay Buhner Haircut Night." As an outfielder for the Mariners, Buhner had hit 25 or more home runs each of the previous three seasons. But Buhner had fewer than 25 strands of hair on his head. He was purely bald. Fans who were willing to have their heads shaved (or who were already lucky enough to be bald) received free admission that night. On that inaugural "Jay Buhner Haircut Night," 512 people got free tickets. Two women and 424 men allowed their heads to be shaved so they could get in free. An additional 86 fans reported to the stadium with no hair.

Was Buhner using steroids? There is no reason to believe he was. The 6'3", 205-pound outfielder hit 21 home runs in 358 at-bats in 1994. By 1996, however, Buhner was able to hit 44 home runs and drive in 138. The bald "haircut," now known as the "Buhner buzz," was gaining popularity. About 3,000 people received free admission during a 1996 Mariners game because they were willing to have their own "Buhner buzz."

Here is the question: does the lack of Buhner's hair prove that Buhner's 44 home runs were steroid induced? Of course not. And everyone seems to understand that. But Buhner was a nice guy, a guy people loved. Barry Bonds, however, is no Jay Buhner. In addition to countless others who hated Bonds because of the way he treated people, Bonds also had to face the *Chronicle*'s best and brightest and an angry woman he had recently dumped after failing to make good on a promise to buy her a house. For the journalists who had Bonds in their sights and the former mistress who wanted revenge, no detail that might support accusations of Bonds's alleged steroid use was too trifling to ignore.

Like almost everything else, irregular hair growth, or even baldness, can be associated with steroid use. Because the impact of steroids is so difficult to measure, there is no convincing scientific evidence that steroid use actually causes baldness. Even if such a study existed, I wouldn't buy it. After all, Governor Schwarzenegger has great hair. And we know he used a few steroids.

But the accusers don't have to worry about Governor Schwarzenegger or professional bodybuilders who have full heads of hair but still make Barry Bonds look like Barry Manilow (in the muscle department, not the hair department). According to the *Shadows* authors, Bonds underwent "physical changes during this time" that "were consistent with steroid use." They say Bonds's "hair fell out, and he began shaving his head." Bell supposedly told the grand jury that when Bonds started losing his hair, "it happened very quickly."

Dr. Harvey Simon explains the current thinking that links balding to hormones:

> A man's scalp is covered by about 100,000 hair follicles, which pass through continual cycles of growth, rest and occasional death. Normally the scalp loses roughly 100 hairs a day and sprouts 100 new ones. But the sex hormone testosterone can upset this break-even dynamic. Testosterone—in the form of DHT, or dihydrotestosterone—stimulates hair growth on the face and the body. But in men who carry a certain common gene, the same hormone gradually defoliates the scalp, causing their aging heads to grow shiny even as their ears, noses and shoulders sprout more hair."

Some common steroids, such as Winstrol, are derived from DHT. This leads to the theory that steroid use can contribute to a balding scalp and excess hair growth in other areas of the body.

There are countless men who lost their hair in their 20s, 30s, and 40s. Although it may be true that a small fraction of the men who lose their hair used steroids, it is equally obvious that the vast majority of men who lose their hair are not taking steroids.

Hair loss has been blamed on everything from genetics (which people cannot control) to frequently wearing a hat (which baseball players do). If Bonds started losing his hair in his mid- to late 30s, that would be perfectly normal. Or maybe Bonds just wanted to sport the increasingly popular shaved-head look. Either way, Bonds's hair (or lack thereof) offers the fair-minded observer nothing of value when it comes to deciding whether or not Bonds used steroids.

Bigfoot? In a paperback version of *Game of Shadows*, the authors include an afterword that implies that Bonds must have been using human growth hormone because his shoe size increased from 10½ to 13. This is another good example of the hysteria that has been devoted to the "Get Bonds" campaign. An increased shoe size does not prove Bonds used HGH. In recent years, people have come to understand that wearing a slightly larger sized shoe is usually more comfortable and better for the foot. But that recognition may not be the only reason Bonds started wearing larger shoes. Dr. Matt Werd, president of the American Academy of Podiatric Sports Medicine, explains: "Keep in mind that foot size will often increase with age, due to a weakening and loosening of the muscles, tendons, and ligaments that hold together the bones and joints in the foot. As our waistline and body weight increases, so does the size of our feet."

Like Williams, Hornsby, Ruth, and Shoeless Joe Jackson, Bonds gained 30 or more pounds over the course of his career. It really would be strange if Bonds still wore the same shoe size he was wearing 20 years ago. But an increased shoe size is perfectly consistent with aging and weight gain. In addition, a two-and-a-half-size increase typically means less than one inch in actual foot elongation. To the extent any part of the increase reflects comfort concerns, as opposed to actual foot expansion, we're talking about an even more minimal expansion.

When this kind of accusation appears without any mention of the facts on aging, weight gain, and shoe size, it comes across as unsubstantiated and a little outlandish. It may be good entertainment, but it isn't the best way to get to the truth.

Unfortunately, the one-sidedness of the attack on Bonds doesn't stop there. According to the *Shadows* afterword, the shoe-size change is important because "medical experts said overuse of human growth hormone could cause an adult's extremities to begin growing." What medical experts? A search of their sources doesn't identify any "medical experts" who are making the claim. Instead, they attribute this shocking information about Bonds's shoe size increase to a guy named Jeff Kranz.

Is Kranz a doctor? No, he's a guy who worked on Wall Street until he started collecting baseball memorabilia full time. Is Kranz a neutral and reliable source? Well, Bonds actually reported Kranz to the FBI, alleging that Kranz was selling fake Bonds memorabilia. So we can't consider him anything close to unbiased. Is it fair for the *Shadows* authors to take Kranz's word for it on the shoe size, not tell readers that Kranz has every reason to try to stick it to Bonds, rely on unnamed medical experts to try to tie increased shoe size to HGH usage, and never mention that shoe size increases naturally with age and weight gain? You tell me.

*

Perhaps the weakest and most shameless indictment of Bonds is based on the argument that his head grew suddenly and dramatically.

There are two basic flaws with the head-size argument. Both sort of jump out at you. First, how do we know that Bonds's head has grown? There are rumors that the Giants started ordering larger hats for Bonds, but Bonds says his hat size has stayed the same—7¼ to 7⅜. Kranz says the Bonds hats he collected were never that big, ranging from 7⅛ to 7¼, but Bonds has accused Kranz of selling counterfeit merchandise. At this point it seems people may be confusing face size with head size. Take a look at before-and-after weight-loss photos. They're easy to find. You will often note that the before photo appears to depict a person with a larger head. The reason is that the before photo depicts a person who weighs more than the person in the after photo. Some of that weight is stored in the face, and it makes the head appear larger.

As he aged, Bonds gained weight. Like many people in his same age class, some of the weight was stored in Bonds's face. With a little more volume in the face, the head can appear somewhat larger. This is the effect that has caused many to jump to the conclusion that Bonds must have been addicted to HGH. Are we so desperate to convict Bonds that we would ask him to try on a 7⅜-size hat in front of the world?

There is a second reason why the head-size argument seems particularly flimsy. As far as we know, none of the attackers is using actual medical evidence to support the claim that adult head size can only increase if one suffers from acromegaly or takes large quantities of HGH. Likewise, even Pearlman's incredibly well-researched book cites no medical studies. This means that, like the other looks arguments, the "his head sure got big" argument rests on a shaky foundation.

6

Those Statistics

Reggie Jackson was a perennial All-Star, a Hall of Famer, an MVP, and baseball's best clutch hitter. His 10 World Series home runs (in just 98 at-bats) earned him the "Mr. October" moniker. He hit 47 home runs in 1969. When Jackson retired in 1987, his 563 home runs placed him behind Hank Aaron, Babe Ruth, Willie Mays, Frank Robinson, and Harmon Killebrew on baseball's all-time home-run list. Jackson's power-hitting skills and unbelievable ability to perform under pressure were exceeded only by his self-promotional capabilities. He still has a high opinion of himself—a fact Jackson's not reluctant to share with others. When Jackson saw players such as Rafael Palmeiro, Sammy Sosa, and Barry Bonds moving ahead of him on the all-time home-run list, he didn't like it.

In 2004 Jackson went public, proclaiming that "somebody definitely is guilty of taking steroids." To Jackson, the proof was in the statistics. The fact that Bonds hit 73 home runs in one season was all the proof Jackson needed. Jackson registered his complaint like this: "I mean, come on now. There is no way you can outperform Aaron and Ruth and Mays at that level." Jackson seemed to take the home runs very personally, to the point that he spoke out even though Major League Baseball had declared the subject off-limits. The gag order didn't stop Jackson:

> There is a reason why the greatest players of all time have
> 500 homers. Then there is that group that is above 550. There
> is a reason for that. Guys played 19, 20, 25 years. They had

113

9,000 to 10,000 at-bats, and it was the same for everybody. Now all of a sudden you are hitting 50 homers when you're 40 years old.

Jackson's point seems to be that a player who excels statistically is proving his own steroid use. Ruth never hit 73 home runs in a season. Mays never hit 73 home runs in the season. Aaron never hit 73 home runs in a season. Therefore, anyone who does must be juicing. If you start with that premise and then assume that no one could have a better season than Ruth, Mays, or Aaron without taking steroids, a player's statistical success becomes self-affirming proof of steroid use.

Jackson's view is certainly understandable. He looked up to the great players who came before him, and he's very proud of his own accomplishments. So he's reluctant to recognize any superiority in today's players. The argument hits home with a lot of us. And it applies to a lot of things—not just baseball or even sports. People of a certain age tend to think most of today's music is terrible when it is compared to the music of the 1970s and 1980s. There are people who think no president could ever be as good as FDR. Stephen Hawking can't possibly be as smart as Albert Einstein. And Pamela Anderson just isn't as attractive as Marilyn Monroe.

It is almost instinctive—we want to defend our favorites, and we want to defend our era. But this is sentimentality, not a legitimate argument. Let's get back to sports. The fact is that the modern athlete is better nourished, better trained, better coached, better motivated, and in many cases, just plain better. It seems people are getting bigger, stronger, and smarter. Compare the 1906 Chicago Cubs infield to the 2006 Yankees infield. The 1906 Cubs dominated, with a remarkable 116–36 record. At first base, Frank Chance was 6', 190 pounds. Second baseman Johnny Evers stood 5'9" and weighed all of 125 pounds. Shortstop Joe Tinker was 5'9" and weighed 175. At third base was

Harry Steinfeldt (the guy no one remembers) at 5'9½" and 180 pounds. The 1906 Cubs' average infielder was shorter than 5'10" and weighed about 168 pounds. The 2006 Yankees won 97 games. Let's put 6'2", 200-pound Jason Giambi at first base. At second, Robinson Cano stands 6' and weighs 170. Shortstop Derek Jeter is a mere 6'3" and 175 pounds. And rounding out the infield is Alex Rodriguez—6'3"and 190 pounds. The average 2006 Yankees infielder stood 6'2"and weighed about 184 pounds.

Aside from the larger size of today's population, there are many more of us. The best and brightest out of 100 million Americans in 1920 are likely to be very good. The best and brightest out of 300 million Americans in 2007 are likely to be substantially better. In fact, each generation of athletes is likely to be better than the last.

Basketball serves as an example of athletic evolution. Fifty years ago there were no 6'9" guards or 7'7" centers to contend with. Changes in player sizes, rules, and styles can make cross-era comparisons challenging. But there's one basketball skill that hasn't changed much over the years: free-throw shooting. Since James Naismith invented the game, the shooter has stood at a line 15 feet away from the hoop, with no defenders to interfere with the shot. A really picky person might argue that free-throw shooting has become slightly more difficult because, if you're playing on the road, people in the seats behind the basket now go crazy making noise and waving things around to try to distract the shooter. Still, free-throw shooting offers a good measure of athletic ability connected to a skill that has remained more or less constant over time.

Bill Sharman was a great basketball player. He was a Hall of Famer. He spent 11 seasons in the National Basketball Association, 10 of those with the Boston Celtics. Sharman's first season in the NBA was 1950–51. He retired following the 1960–61 season. Sharman was generally considered the best free-throw shooter of his era. He was almost twice as good at shooting free throws as Shaquille O'Neal.

Sharman retired with a .883 free-throw percentage. His best year was 1958–59, when he made 342 of the 367 free throws he attempted—a .932 success rate.

So how does an extraordinary talent like Sharman stack up against the best shooters from subsequent generations? The answer is, not bad. He's 10th on the all-time free-throw shooting percentage list. Not surprisingly, however, several of the players who rank ahead of Sharman are still active. After the 2006–07 season ended, Steve Nash was number three on the list. His free-throw percentage was .897. Peja Stojakovic was number four on the list (.892). The all-time best free-throw shooter is Mark Price, who retired in 1998. Of the players who have better free-throw percentages than Sharman, Rick Barry is the most antiquated, having retired in 1980. But Barry's .900 accuracy may not be a fair comparison because he was smart enough to use the "granny" style so many current NBA players *should* be using.

The point is that athletes in general are getting better. Price wasn't on steroids. Nash isn't on steroids. They just happen to be a little bit better at shooting free throws than Sharman was. If Bonds became a bit more adept at hitting home runs than some of baseball's icons were, it doesn't mean he used steroids. It just means he was better at hitting home runs. Sorry, Mr. October.

Before we search for statistical evidence that Bonds hit all those home runs because he used steroids, we might as well try to get a handle on *when* he allegedly started using all those steroids. There are at least two competing schools of thought. José Canseco traces Bonds's use of steroids to sometime in 2000. Canseco says Bonds was awed by Canseco's muscularity during the February 2000, big-league challenge in Las Vegas, Nevada, and it wasn't just the muscle. Bonds had to watch Canseco win the home run–hitting contest.

Canseco's theory seems to be that Bonds started using steroids the next off-season—after the 2000 season ended and before the 2001 season started. Canseco says Bonds "showed up in spring 2001 with 40 pounds of added muscle."

Canseco's observations fit the "one-season wonder" view. This view seems to be that Bonds went on steroids after the 2000 season ended and managed to get huge just in time for the 2001 season to start. He then went out and hit 73 home runs in 476 at-bats. But, according to Jeff Pearlman, by the time 2002 rolled around, Bonds looked "significantly smaller than he had toward the end of the 2001 season, when he weighed a reported 228 pounds."

But others who accuse Bonds say he started using steroids earlier, after the 1998 season—after he was forced to watch Mark McGwire smack 70 home runs and Sammy Sosa slam 66. Of course, to make this theory work it would be nice if Canseco's home run–hitting contest at Cashman Field in Las Vegas had taken place in 1997 or 1998, rather than 2000. The temptation to try to squeeze the facts to fit the theory may have been too much for Howard Bryant. In his otherwise excellent book, *Juicing the Game*, Bryant tells us that the encounter between Bonds and Canseco at the Las Vegas home-run Derby took place in 1997. That would certainly be welcome news for those who want to accuse Bonds of using steroids as early as 1998. But it is not accurate. Believe it or not, Canseco's book accurately reported that the encounter occurred in February 2000, not in 1997. Imagine that, the accusers can't even agree on when Bonds started hitting the juice!

Let's focus on the one truly anomalous year—2001—when Bonds hit .328, with 73 home runs in just 476 at-bats. Were these statistics so anomalous that they qualify as proof of steroid use? No doubt, the numbers *are* awe inspiring. That year, Bonds hit 24 more home runs than he hit in any other season. He hit a home run every 6.5 at-bats, a ratio nearly twice as good as anyone had a right to expect based on Bonds's performances between 1986 and 2000. There were other seasons in which Bonds had managed to produce a higher batting average. For example, in 1993 Bonds had hit .336, with 46 home runs. Still, against the rest of Bonds's career statistics, the unbelievable barrage of 73 home runs sticks out like a sore thumb.

Is the one-season home-run spike proof of steroid use? We have already looked at Roger Maris's 1961 season, when Maris hit 61 home runs, and concluded that it was more statistically anomalous than Bonds's 2001 season. Are there any other one-season wonders who might provide insight as to whether Bonds must have been on steroids in 2001? I'm glad you asked.

Dave Kingman was a lanky former USC Trojan. At 6'6" and 210 pounds, Kingman had the stature of a home-run hitter. He had a "swing for the fences" approach to hitting that generated more than 1,800 career strikeouts in fewer than 6,700 career at-bats. Kingman's lifetime batting average was .236. Kingman had "good" years in which he hit less than .240, and some years that saw him hit under .210. He may not have made contact often, but when he did, he drove the ball.

Before 1979 Kingman had two very good years. In 1975 he hit 36 home runs, while batting .231. In 1976 Kingman hit 37 home runs, while batting .238. The 1977 season was an off year, and Kingman hit just .221, with 26 home runs, while playing for four different teams. The following season Kingman's average ticked up to .266, and he hit a respectable 28 home runs. Then came the big year—1979. Suddenly, Kingman was on fire for the Chicago Cubs. He hit a career-high 48 home runs and had his best batting average ever (.288). After that, Kingman was never able to post similar numbers. In 1982 he did hit 37 home runs, but his average was a mere .204. So, for Kingman, 1979 was a monster year. He hit 11 more home runs than he hit in any other year, and he also had his best-ever batting average, an average that exceeded his average in some of his "good" years by more than

80 points. Not one person blamed Kingman's 1979 surge on steroids or HGH.

Andre Dawson had a great career, combining 314 stolen bases with 438 home runs. He was a top-notch outfielder, mostly for the Montreal Expos and the Chicago Cubs. He won eight Gold Glove awards. As a 28-year-old in 1983, Dawson had his best season to that point. He hit 32 home runs and drove in 113. Over the next three seasons, Dawson hit 60 home runs. The best of those three seasons was 1985, when he hit 23 home runs. Then, suddenly, as a 32-year-old, Dawson had an MVP season in 1987, when he slammed 49 home runs for the Chicago Cubs. After that, Dawson played another nine years for the Cubs, Red Sox, and Marlins. But he would never again hit as many as 32 home runs in any other season. Excluding 1987, Dawson averaged 19.45 home runs per year. The 49 homers he smashed in 1987 were about two and a half times his average, and they represented a 50 percent increase over his next best season.

In some ways Dawson's 1987 was comparable to Bonds's 2001. And we can be reasonably certain Dawson was not using steroids. It is not particularly difficult to identify players who had a single season that "graphs out" like Bonds's 2001—that one year where, at least from a home run standpoint, everything fell into place.

Gabby Hartnett was a Hall of Fame catcher who played 20 years in the National League between 1922 and 1941. Hartnett connected for 37 home runs in 1930. His next best season total was in 1925, when he hit 24 home runs. Excluding 1930, Hartnett averaged only about 10 home runs per season.

Davey Lopes, the longtime second baseman for the Los Angeles Dodgers, had a 1979 season that was hard to explain. During his first six full seasons with the Dodgers, Lopes had averaged fewer than 10 home runs per year. In 1979 Lopes suddenly exploded for 28 home runs. Before 1979 Lopes had never hit more than 17 home runs in a single season. Lopes played eight more years in the major leagues, but he never hit more than 17 home runs in any of those seasons. Lopes ultimately played 16 seasons and hit 155 home runs. A full 18 percent of the home runs Lopes hit throughout his entire career came during that one season in 1979. In contrast, the 73 home runs Bonds hit in 2001 account for less than 10 percent of his career home-run total.

If Lopes were playing today and producing the same statistical pattern, he would probably be accused of using steroids. Because Lopes played long before any major league players were even allegedly using steroids, there must be alternative explanations for the single-season home-run explosion. But let's face it—it isn't 1979 anymore, and now it's a lot easier to accuse players who have a sudden productivity increase of using steroids.

One more example really forces us to question whether it makes any sense to try to blame Bonds's 73-home-run season on steroids. We know Davey Johnson never used steroids. Johnson was a 6'1" second baseman who weighed 180 pounds. He played in the major leagues for 13 seasons, between 1965 and 1978. From 1965 through 1972, Johnson had 3,489 at-bats, and he hit a grand total of 66 home runs. In other words, Johnson hit a home run every 52.86 at-bats. His home-run percentage was minuscule—less than 2 percent.

Before 1973, Johnson's highest single-season home-run total was 18. But something happened in 1973. We don't know what it was, but we know it wasn't steroids. In 1973 Johnson blasted 43 home runs. He did it in just 559 at-bats, a home-run percentage of 7.7 percent—a home run every 13 at-bats. Johnson played until 1978, hitting a grand total of 27 home runs after 1973.

Johnson's 13 big-league seasons produced a total of 136 home runs. An amazing 31.6 percent of those home runs were hit during that one year in 1973. Johnson is living proof that a baseball player can suddenly achieve a measure of success that comes out of nowhere, a measure of success that may be hard to explain but is not steroid induced. If Johnson had produced his statistics during the 1990s and 2000s, rather than in the 1960s and 1970s, he would be considered "Exhibit A" by those who believe sudden home-run success is a product of steroid use.

Bonds's antagonists have a hard time getting around the fact that hot streaks and hard-to-explain statistical spikes are part of the game. Many players who were not even arguably steroid users have achieved statistical improvements that seemed to be even more outlandish than Bonds's 73 home runs. So the argument needs to be refined. And the refinement is that Bonds was 36 years old when he hit the 73 home runs. Because Bonds was in his mid-30s when his home-run rate improved so dramatically, he had to be on steroids.

Even the refined argument overlooks several factors that help explain the success Bonds was able to achieve at an age when some baseball players are no longer able to perform. Most significantly, Bonds's success largely coincides with the aggressive workout and weight-training regimen that he started in the 1990s. Through extreme training Bonds was able to stay in shape at an age when other players are growing soft. He was also able to increase his strength.

In a way, comparing Bonds to players from prior generations is like comparing apples to oranges. The Phillies' legendary third baseman Mike Schmidt played from 1972 to 1989. He was inducted into the Hall of Fame in 1995 after a career that included 548 home runs. Schmidt was a relatively hard worker, and he was very productive into his late 30s. In 1987, when he was 37, Schmidt hit 35 home runs, drove in 113, and batted .293. But Schmidt belonged to a generation of players that didn't take care of their bodies as well as many current players do. Schmidt describes the times by saying, "I can't tell you how many nights I drove home from a game with four beers in me and another two in a bag on the seat. Many nights I'd get home and not even remember the drive."

Schmidt belonged to a generation that drank (and in many cases, smoked) itself into early retirement. You don't need a medical degree to understand that players who drink heavily and enjoy tobacco too often face challenges in trying to maintain the peak physical condition that is required to achieve success at the highest level of professional athletics.

Bonds doesn't smoke, and he drinks only on rare occasions. And that makes a big difference. Mickey Mantle liked to drink. He hit 35 home runs with a .303 average in 1964 when he was 32 years old. After that, it was all downhill. When he was 33, Mantle hit .255 (with only 19 home runs). The next year he hit .288, then .245, and finally, .237 when he retired at age 36. If you enjoy yourself too much along the way, you probably are not going to be a productive major leaguer at age 40. But Bonds has never really enjoyed himself much, let alone too much. That's why it makes no sense to assume that Bonds was on steroids just because he had great seasons at an age that had other players thinking about retirement.

Is there a certain age when the body just breaks down? Is there a certain age when outstanding performance is impossible without assistance from performance-enhancing drugs? If so, what is that age—33? How old is too old—35? When does the body break down—at 37? The truth is that not everyone ages at the same rate or in the same way. Long before anyone was accused of using steroids there were baseball players who managed to have their best years after they had reached a chronological age at which many of their peers retired.

Zack Wheat played 19 seasons, mostly as an outfielder for the Brooklyn Dodgers. In 1919 Wheat was 31 years old and should have been in his physical prime. That year Wheat hit .297, with only five home runs and 62 RBIs. He enjoyed his best season six years later, in

1925. The 37-year-old Wheat should have been a mere shadow of his 31-year-old self. But next to the young man, the old man looked like Superman. Wheat hit .359 in 1925. And the 37-year-old was suddenly a slugger, slamming 14 home runs, 14 triples, and 42 doubles. Although Wheat's brother Mack was out of the majors by the time he was 28, Zack managed to drive in 103 runs when he was 37 years old.

Jake Daubert started his career as a relatively light-hitting first baseman. Daubert played a total of 15 seasons. While he was in his prime, between the ages of 26 and 37, Daubert hit a total of 41 home runs—an average of 3.4 per year. Something happened when he turned 38. Suddenly, in 1922, Daubert had power. He hit 12 home runs that year, more than three times his annual average. His .336 batting average was his highest in nine years. And Daubert's 22 triples and 114 runs scored were both career highs.

Did Ted Williams start taking steroids in 1957? Williams was always a great player, but it had been a long time since he hit .406 in 1941 at the age of 22. And as he entered his 30s, Williams's productivity seemed to be on the decline. He hit .317 and .318 in 1950 and 1951. Those were good averages for most players, but not for Williams. Then, his home-run totals stagnated. Between 1950 and 1956 Williams never hit more than 30 home runs in a season. No one would have suspected that the 38-year-old Williams would hit better than the 27-year-old Williams, but that is exactly what happened. In 1957 Williams smashed 38 home runs and hit .388. His on-base percentage was .526. Although he was closing in on age 40, Williams managed to draw 119 walks, against only 43 strikeouts. Obviously, Williams was not on steroids, he was just a great hitter who happened to be getting older. And while Williams had certainly gained weight during his career, no one blamed steroids.

Darrell Evans was not a great hitter, but he was certainly good. Altogether, Evans played 21 seasons for the Braves, Giants, and Tigers, mostly at third base. Evans had his best season as a 26-year-old. In

1973 he hit 41 home runs for the Atlanta Braves. The next nine seasons Evans was comparatively quiet—he averaged less than 18 home runs during those nine years.

Suddenly, when he turned 36, Evans had a resurgence. He belted 30 home runs in 1983 as a 36-year-old. He played a little less and managed to hit "only" 16 home runs at age 37. Then, as a 38-year-old first baseman for the Detroit Tigers, Evans crushed 40 home runs. Two seasons later the 40-year-old Evans hit 34 home runs and finished a very respectable 12th in MVP voting, ahead of Robin Yount, Roger Clemens, and Canseco. No one accused Evans of using steroids. He just happened to find his power stroke after he turned 36, the same age Bonds was when he hit 73 home runs.

Carlton Fisk is a Hall of Fame catcher who played 24 seasons for the Boston Red Sox and the Chicago White Sox. During the first half of his career, Fisk's best power year was 1977, when he was 29 years old. Fisk slugged 26 home runs and drove in 102. During the next seven seasons, Fisk averaged 16.5 home runs a year.

Something happened in 1985, when Fisk turned a whopping 37 years old. During the prior off-season, Fisk worked out like a madman, using Nautilus machines. When spring training started, Fisk was in great shape. Four months into the season his 29 home runs already established a career high. His pace slowed over the last two months, but he still hit eight more home runs, bringing his season total to 37. The 37-year-old Fisk had used weight training to hit 11 more home runs than he hit in any other season. He drove in 107 runs (his career best), and stole 17 bases (tying his career high). Fisk was not on steroids; he had used weight training to increase his strength and productivity.

Fisk's home-run pace slowed during the second half of the season because, unlike Bonds, Fisk did not continue working out while the season was ongoing. (Fisk caught 130 games that year. Compared to a position such as left field, catching is far more physically taxing. Maintaining an in-season workout regimen might have been particularly difficult for a catcher.) His strength started to decline during the season's second half.

The connection between Fisk's off-season workouts and his dramatic power surge was so direct and convincing that it prompted Sandy Alderson to hire Dave McKay as the first strength and conditioning coach for the Oakland A's. McKay was soon working with players such as Canseco and McGwire. The rest is history.

A close examination of the statistical "evidence" reveals that Bonds's outstanding performance is not compelling evidence of steroid use. Instead, we can find other examples of players who were not using steroids, yet had outstanding seasons (or clusters of outstanding seasons) in their late 30s, just as Bonds did. And we can find other players who suddenly had a season (or a string of seasons) that looked vastly superior to their "normal" performance, even though we know those players never used steroids. In fact, Bonds's outstanding performance from 2000 to 2004 seems substantially less remarkable because Bonds was a National League MVP as early as 1990, when the 25-year-old Pirate hit 33 home runs, drove in 114 runs, and stole 52 bases, all while batting .301.

When we consider where Bonds started, his 73 home runs in 2001 are not as shocking as Johnson's 73—well, the 43 home runs Johnson hit in 1973. And the late-career productivity Bonds managed to generate seems even less suspect when we consider his unparalleled dedication to the game, his singular drive to become the greatest baseball player ever, and the rigorous weight training that Bonds was willing to endure. In short, the plentiful supply of players who obviously never used steroids but managed to create tremendous upside statistical anomalies and late-career surges is a constant reminder that the statistical success Bonds enjoyed doesn't come close to proving that Bonds used steroids.

But wait, there's more. This statistical "evidence" doesn't account for the many ways baseball has changed over the years, meaning comparing the old-time legends with modern players is not valid. This omission is doubly confounding because almost all of the changes inexorably lead to more offensive productivity and more home runs.

*

Perhaps the one man who did more than anyone else to facilitate all those home runs that Bonds hit was Mr. Mays. No, not Willie Mays—Carl Mays. Mays was born in 1891. He made his major league debut as a pitcher in 1915, and he had his best season in 1921, with the Yankees. That year, Mays won 27 games, lost only nine, and had an earned-run average of 3.05.

Nevertheless, Mays was a troubled man. One day in 1919, when he was with the Boston Red Sox, he was enjoying a game as a virtual spectator while a teammate was pitching against Philadelphia. The crowd was apparently fairly big and perhaps a little unruly. They were, after all, in Philadelphia. A big part of the crowd had gathered primarily to watch Mays's teammate, Ruth. It was only the second inning when Philadelphia generated three runs, and the fans got excited because the Athletics had taken a 3–2 lead. A group of fans started pounding on the tin roof that sat atop the visiting dugout. For the players inside the dugout, the noise must have been hellish. One player—Mays—decided to do something about it. He jumped out of the dugout holding a baseball. He wound up and hurled the ball into the stands. (What would Ron Artest have done?) The ball grazed a woman's head, then hit Bryan Hayes. Luckily for Hayes, he was wearing a straw hat that partially cushioned the blow. Still, Hayes decided to visit the police station and press charges against Mays.

Mays had anger-management issues. And, perhaps because he pitched with a virtually underhanded delivery, he also sometimes had trouble throwing strikes. Mays threw the pitch—the pitch that was to change the balance of power in favor of future generations of hitters—on August 16, 1920.

Like Bonds, Ray Chapman once stole 52 bases in a single season. And that is where the similarities end. Chapman spent his entire nine-season major league career with the Cleveland Indians. He was the most popular player on the team, always in a good mood. In the days before boom boxes and iPods, Chapman liked to keep his teammates loose by singing, laughing, and joking.

It was 1916 when Chapman met Kathleen Daly, daughter of millionaire oil man Martin B. Daly. Chapman had been playing for the Cleveland Indians since 1912, and as his relationship with Ms. Daly blossomed, her father urged Chapman to quit baseball to become a full-time business leader. In fact, Daly got Chapman a job as the secretary treasurer of Pioneer Alloys Company. Chapman figured he would have plenty of time for business when his baseball days were over, so he kept playing baseball and he kept dating Kathleen. Finally, on October 29, 1919, Kathleen and Chapman were married. Chapman had come a long way. Born in a small Kentucky town, the son of a coal miner, Chapman had achieved success in baseball and married into a family situation that promised even greater prosperity once his playing days were over.

Still practically a newlywed, Chapman got off to a reasonably good start in 1920. About two-thirds of the way through the season he had hit three home runs (tying his career high) and stolen 13 bases, while hitting .303. He had already scored 97 runs in his first 111 games.

It was hot and humid in New York on August 16, 1920. Chapman's Indians were playing Mays's Yankees, and the two teams were locked in the middle of a tight pennant race. In his first at-bat against Mays, Chapman bunted to move a runner over. He tried to bunt again in his next at-bat, but he popped the ball up and Wally Pipp managed to turn a double play. Chapman's next at-bat was in the top of the fifth inning. In the middle of his windup, Mays thought he saw Chapman shift his weight, as if he were going to bunt again (even though no one was on base). In a fraction of a second, Mays decided to throw the ball high and tight to minimize the likelihood of a successful bunt. Mays's submarine-style pitching caused the ball to keep rising as it traveled toward home plate. The pitch was flying right toward Chapman, who temporarily froze.

The baseball rocketed into Chapman's left temple with so much force that many of the 23,000 fans in attendance assumed the loud "crack" they had heard was the ball hitting the bat. Unfortunately, their assumption was wrong. Like the fans, Mays also thought the ball had hit the bat. He picked it up and threw to first base to make sure he got the out. For a second or two, Chapman had stood at the plate, but now he was slowly crumpling to the ground. The umpire saw blood streaming from Chapman's left ear, so he raced to the stands and called for a doctor. Now, players from both teams were rushing to home plate to offer their assistance. The Indians' player-manager, Tris Speaker, had to bark at the players to stand back so Chapman could get some air.

Chapman tried to speak, but he was unable to form words. Amazingly, after some ice was applied to his head, he was able to stand and walk toward the clubhouse. But before Chapman could get far, his knees gave out. He was carried the rest of the way and then rushed to a hospital as soon as an ambulance could arrive. In the clubhouse, while waiting for the ambulance, Chapman again tried to communicate. The Indians' trainer struggled to understand what Chapman was trying to say. Finally, he understood. Chapman was calling for the wedding ring he had removed before the game started. When the trainer located the ring and placed it on Chapman's finger, Chapman calmed down.

At the hospital, things didn't look so good. X-rays revealed that Chapman had sustained a major fracture, running almost four inches to the base of his skull. A piece of bone was pressing against his brain. Nevertheless, Chapman managed to speak to John Henry, a close friend who had traveled from Boston to watch the game. Chapman told Henry, "For God's sake, don't call [Kathleen], but if you do, tell her I'm all right." Those were the last words Ray Chapman ever spoke.

An emergency surgery helped only temporarily, and Chapman died just before 5:00 in the morning on Tuesday, August 17, 1920. The 29-year-old Chapman was the first—and so far—only, fatality suffered from on-field major league baseball activity.

Mays's killer pitch changed everything. With Mays's teammate, Ruth, making the game more profitable, the owners could now afford to make the game safer for hitters. In fact, even before Chapman died, baseball was inching toward making batters safer. In 1919 the rules had been modified to minimize "freak pitches"—pitches where something was applied or done to the baseball to change its shape, texture, or surface. The rule change eliminated most spitballs, shine balls, Emory balls, and licorice balls. Still, in 1920 each team was allowed to designate two spitball pitchers, as long as those pitchers were known to use the spitball previously.

With Chapman's death, the league had to make the game safer for hitters. The most immediate post-Chapman rule change involved the frequency of introducing new baseballs into a game. Before the horrific incident, umpires were pressured to use baseballs economically, if not parsimoniously. Ironically, Mays himself pointed out the umpires' extreme reluctance to replace old baseballs with new ones the prior season. During a trip to Cleveland, Mays had lost (or someone had stolen) his glove. Since Mays was scheduled to start that afternoon, he ran out hurriedly to buy a new glove and oiled it heavily to help break it in. Mays oiled the new glove excessively—the excess oil made the game ball slippery and hard to hold. Nevertheless, when Mays asked the umpire, Ollie Chill, for a new baseball, Chill denied his request and said nothing was wrong with the slippery ball.

The prevailing view was that the ball that hit Chapman had been in play too long. It had become worn and dark—difficult to see. This view receives support from the notion that Chapman had stood at the plate and froze, as if he lost sight of the ball. So, baseball's dead-ball era was officially over, ended with a single deadly pitch. Never again would a player like Frank Baker (who stood 5'11" and weighed all of 173 pounds), with a lifetime single-season home-run best of 12, sport the nickname "Home Run." Ever since Chapman's death, umpires closely scrutinize the baseball. Ever since that one pitch, umpires have been ready, willing, and able to replace a damaged or dirty ball with a fresh, clean, white one. By the 1970s, a player like Reggie Jackson merely had to ask the umpire to inspect the ball. Now, it is virtually automatic—umpires remove balls that hit the dirt. Today's players don't even have to ask.

Over the next eight decades baseball would remain timeless in many ways, and yet, it would also undergo many small (some, almost imperceptible) changes that would pave the way for single-season and career home-run totals that made the old records seem rather modest. All of these changes combined to make statistical comparisons especially unlikely to produce valuable evidence of any particular player's use of steroids. All of these changes made it more likely that a supertalent such as Bonds would have a season in which everything fell in place and records were shattered. All of these changes made it more likely that a supertalent with longevity and durability, such as Bonds or Alex Rodriguez (30 years old with 464 career home runs), could seriously think about hitting 800 or more home runs in a career.

During the at-bat that ended his life, Chapman was wearing a soft cloth cap. Better head protection almost certainly would have saved his life. Believe it or not, it took another two decades for major league players to start wearing batting helmets. After he was hit in the head in 1907, Roger Bresnahan briefly wore a head-protection device. But he was mocked in the press, and the idea did not catch on. By the 1940s some teams were requiring their players to wear protective head gear.

Although helmets were not mandated until the late 1950s, the Chapman incident certainly paved the way for the use of modern batting helmets. In its immediate aftermath, baseball's owners started discussing the possibility of players wearing headgear like the leather helmets football players were starting to wear. Within a few days of Chapman's death, *The New York Times* made an effort to point out that virtually all safety equipment was initially ridiculed, subsequently popularized, and finally, virtually mandated. The shin guards Hall of Fame catcher Roger Bresnahan—the same player who briefly tried protective headgear—first donned in the 1900s offer the perfect example. Although his shin guards were initially the subject of jokes and negative comments, it wasn't long before all catchers were wearing them.

After attending the University of California, Darren Lewis played parts of 13 seasons in the major leagues, mostly with the Giants and Red Sox. Lewis was a light-hitting speedster who stole 46 bases for the Giants in 1993. But it was the next season, 1994, when Lewis may have inadvertently helped to push Bonds to the next level. Lewis couldn't suggest improvements to Bonds's batting stance, swing, or mental approach to hitting. Instead, Lewis helped Bonds by running into him at full speed.

With Bonds in left and Lewis in center, Luis Gonzalez of the Houston Astros drove the ball to deep left-center field. Bonds and Lewis both gave chase—a chase that ended in a violent collision. Bonds landed with most of his weight on his right elbow. For a while, Bonds had no feeling in his right hand. The elbow was iced, and Bonds left the clubhouse after the game with an elbow pad he planned to wear both on and off the field.

Within a few weeks Bonds's elbow pad had morphed into a piece of the body armor that seems to make Bonds appear invincible at the plate. When the Giants beat the Cardinals, 10–3, on June 5, 1994, the *San Francisco Chronicle*'s Tim Keown explained the elbow pad like this:

> Bonds was 3 for 3, and he's standing in there like a guy ready for a serious tear. He's all pumped up about the new elbow pad he's wearing, and the Giants figure whatever makes him happy makes them happy.
>
> The pad, which he started wearing Saturday, is made of hard plastic, but it's flexible. It was created from a mold of his right arm, and it allows him full extension on his swing. It also gives him the confidence to stand in there and wait until the last millisecond, something he hasn't been able to do.

Does the body armor make a difference? Through the 1994 season, when Bonds started wearing more protection, he hit 259 home runs in 4,514 at-bats, a home-run percentage of approximately 5.7 percent. From 1995 through 2006, aided by body armor, Bonds hit 475 home runs in 4,993 at-bats—a home-run percentage of approximately 9.5 percent. We know the body armor made Bonds happy, and we know his home-run percentage improved. But should we really believe that wearing some protective plastic can significantly improve the hitter's output?

In *Clearing the Bases*, Mike Schmidt offers seven specific reasons why Bonds is "the best hitter in baseball history—period." Describing one of those seven reasons, Schmidt explains:

> Finally—and this may seem trivial, but it's not—Bonds takes full advantage of subtle changes in the rules of the

game over the past decade.... Bonds wears an elbow guard,
which 20 years ago would not have been allowed. It shields
his front side from inside fastballs, functioning as a security
blanket that makes him more comfortable at the plate.

Schmidt sees the body armor as a significant weapon in the
psychological battle between pitcher and hitter. As Schmidt explains,
"If a batter doesn't have in the back of his mind that he could get
one in the neck for taking liberties with the pitcher's sense of what's
rightfully his, he starts the at-bat with an advantage. It's like starting
a golf match one-up before you even tee off." Schmidt goes on to
explain that Bonds "knows he intimidates every pitcher he faces. As
so much of the pitcher-hitter confrontation is psychological, he enjoys
a huge edge the second he steps into the batter's box."

Joe Morgan is a broadcaster who also happened to be a great second
baseman and a very good hitter. Inducted into baseball's Hall of Fame
in 1990, Morgan was a mere 5'7" and 160 pounds during his playing
days. Still, he managed to hit 268 home runs during a career that also
included 689 stolen bases. Morgan knows something about generating
power as a hitter. He points out that "good hitters...stand close to the
plate." Because pitchers were typically throwing at the outside corner,
hitters tended to move in toward the plate. According to Morgan, many
"adjusted their style and began diving in toward the plate." Morgan
says pitchers have tried to adjust, too. They have tried to use the inside
part of the plate more often. But, Morgan says, "Today's hitters will
turn and let the ball hit them in the back, in the arm—and sometimes
in the helmet. Because hitters know they're more likely to get hit, they
have begun wearing body armor to protect themselves."

Some people who may not know whether using steroids can
make a person a better hitter offer some pretty strong feelings about
body armor and its ability to make hitters more comfortable and more
effective at the plate. Jeff Zillgitt didn't hold back, explaining:

Might as well just give San Francisco Giants home-run master Barry Bonds shoulder pads and a face mask, too. Bonds already wears a hard plastic shell (known in baseball circles as armor) on his right elbow, allowing him to hover as close to home plate as he wishes without fear of getting hurt if a Curt Schilling fastball drills him in the elbow.

Zillgitt even credits the body armor with shrinking Bonds's strike zone:

> And by crowding the plate, Bonds consciously or subconsciously shrinks the umpire's strike zone. Bonds has drawn 128 walks this year, most in the league and fourth-highest total in his career. He walked at least 100 times in nine of the last 12 seasons. Credit more than a handful of those bases on balls to a small strike zone created by Bonds's ability to crowd the plate with little worry about getting pegged on the funny bone.

Pitcher David Wells unwittingly disclosed the impact of body armor on the pitcher's psyche when he said that one way "to earn yourself that scarlet A" is to "cover your arms with 17 pieces of Kevlar padding and then have the balls to stand on top of home plate. If ever there was a reason to plant a baseball-size bruise on a guy's ass, this is it."

Many people believe steroid use cannot help a baseball player become a more successful hitter. It is, after all, hard to ignore the Canseco brothers. They have similar genetic gifts, to put it mildly. They are twins. Both used steroids. José hit 462 home runs and stole 200 bases during his career. Ozzie had no home runs and stole no bases during his career.

Yet, many of the same people who believe steroids cannot make hitters better also believe that body armor *can* significantly improve hitting statistics. And some want to see body armor eliminated from the game. Criticisms range from the unnatural, if not unfair, advantage armored hitters receive, to the increasing frequency of hitters intentionally allowing the ball to hit them because the physical consequences are so minimal when armor is employed.

Mark Prior is a 6'5", 225-pound power pitcher. He had been dominant in college when he pitched for the USC Trojans, and he was just as dominant for the Chicago Cubs in 2003. Prior won 18 games that year and lost only six. He struck out 245 batters in just 211 innings. His earned-run average was just 2.43. In May 2003, Prior squared off with Bonds. He drilled Bonds in the hip. Bonds took a few steps toward Prior, and a little verbal exchange ensued, but cooler heads prevailed. After the game, Prior told his side of the story:

> He said what he had to say, and I said what I had to say. I'm sure he's mad, rightfully so, but I'm not backing down. He can get mad all he wants. Just because he's been around 15 years doesn't mean I don't have to do my job with him up there. I need the inside of the plate to be effective.... He's an intimidator. It's part of his game, but it's also part of mine. He's standing at the plate wearing armor. I have no problem with that; if they want to strap up the armor, fine. I wear a cup. That's all I need.

Cup versus body armor, and everyone lived to tell about it.

Other changes in equipment have also made hitting home runs easier while making meaningful statistical comparisons across eras more difficult. Perhaps the most important equipment change involves the ball itself. People believed baseballs got livelier during the 1920s. Introduction of the cork-center ball and material shortages during World War I are credited for much of the increase in home runs the 1920s and 1930s witnessed. More probably, it was the elimination of "freak" pitches, more frequent substitution of new baseballs into the games, and bigger, stronger players taking "home-run" swings that generated increases in the number of home runs.

If the 1960s were pitching-dominant years, and the 1970s and 1980s were "normal" years, there is no denying the apparent increase in home runs that seemed to materialize during the late 1980s. George F. Will, the political commentator, passed along this theory to explain the sudden increase in home runs:

> In 1987 a sudden increase in home runs produced the "Happy Haitian" explanation: baseballs were then manufactured in Haiti, and the theory was that the fall of the Duvalier regime so inspired Haitians that they worked with more pep, pulling the stitching tighter, thereby flattening the seams—and flattening curveballs. The smoother balls had less wind resistance to give them movement when pitched, or to slow their subsequent flight over outfielders.

Okay, okay. That does sound like someone was using drugs—something a little stronger than steroids. When Will and his sources talk about the qualities of baseballs, we can easily disregard the commentary as provocative but ill-informed. (As Ted Williams once said, "I like George Will politically, but baseballically, he was all wrong.") On the other hand, when Schmidt tells us about lively baseballs, his comments can't be dismissed so easily. Schmidt is convinced that the modern baseball is "wound a little tighter, is a little harder, has slightly flatter seams, and is a little more consistent." He says the differences are "not much, but enough to matter, enough to make it harder, enough to make it travel slightly farther."

Others saw even bigger differences in the ball. Pitcher David Wells complained that the balls were so tight that he could not get a proper grip. This made his curveball particularly inconsistent. Wells also complained about how smooth the balls were. He estimated that only one in 10 had seams that were sufficiently raised so that he could generate favorable rotation on his pitches.

Billy Sample had played outfield for the Texas Rangers, New York Yankees, and Atlanta Braves during the 1970s and 1980s. Sample joked that if the balls were any harder the manufacturer would have to put the word "Titleist" on them.

Just a few years ago, Schmidt managed in the minor leagues. He describes his experience like this:

> I threw batting practice for five straight months, and I believe in my heart that the current balls are slightly tighter, and ever so slightly smaller. So while there are other significant reasons for the offensive boom of the last decade, I believe there is no question that the baseball, that little 5.25-ounce sphere we all cherish so much, is—as it always has been in a situation like this—a likely suspect.

Seventy-three home runs. A smaller, lighter, livelier ball with flatter seams may explain some of those home runs. What about the bat? Well, bats have changed, too. Old-school thinking was that a hitter who could use a heavier bat was better off, all else being equal. Babe Ruth sometimes used a bat that weighed 54 ounces. As late as the 1980s, some of the game's most prolific home-run hitters used bats that were heavy enough to fill the role of a weighted warm-up bat for most of today's players. Today's sluggers understand that bat speed is king. The lighter the bat, the faster the swing. If the swing is swifter, the batter has more time to assess the pitch. More time to assess the pitch should translate to fewer swings at bad pitches, more walks, and more offensive productivity. At 6'4" and 230 pounds, the Phillies' Ryan Howard is bigger than Ruth. Howard uses a 34-ounce bat.

Sam Holman is a carpenter by trade. In 1989 he sustained a serious leg injury while playing basketball. The injury ultimately forced him out of his job. As a result, Sam had time to devote himself to a challenge he had received from a friend and professional baseball scout—come up with a bat that won't break. Most wood bats were made from ash. The wood was lightweight, but not particularly sturdy or strong. Maple wood could make a stronger bat, but air-dried maple would be too heavy. With new kiln-drying techniques, however, maple could now be processed in a superior way, so that it was both stronger and more durable, on the one hand, and lighter, on the other. The end result is Holman's Canadian company, a company that identifies itself as "The Original Maple Bat Company."

Joe Carter is said to be the first major league player to use the maple "Sam Bat" in a game. It was 1997. The Sam Bat was revolutionary, not just because it resisted breaking but also because of what it did to the ball. Major league hitters touted the bat's hardness and lauded its durability. They also noted that Sam Bats are "definitely heavier on impact." Carter summed it up: "When you first use [a Sam Bat], it's a total different feel from a normal bat…. I mean totally different. After you use [a Sam Bat] you don't want to go back."

When Ralph Kiner tried to explain the home-run surge that started in the mid-1990s, he said, "No one talks about the newer bats. They should, because they might be the biggest factor of all." In 2002 Schmidt proved Kiner's point when he competed in a Philadelphia Phillies alumni home-run contest before a game at Veterans Stadium. Schmidt wasn't exactly in baseball shape. He had turned 50 two years earlier. Schmidt was actually a bit reluctant to participate because he thought he might not hit a single home run. But someone gave Schmidt a Sam Bat to use during the competition. This is how Schmidt described his experience with the Sam Bat:

> Have you ever hit a golf ball with a baseball bat? That's the best way I can describe the feeling. If this little exhibition had taken place in 1980, with the equipment of that era but using my swing of 2002, maybe one ball would have left the park. There is *no way* that the combination of the maple Sam Bat and the current baseball didn't add a minimum of 10 to 20 feet to the flight of the ball. I hadn't touched a bat in five years, and in 10 swings, this stiff, fifty-something old-timer hit four balls over the fence—and in the first deck—at Veterans Stadium. And I was just getting warmed up.

The steroid conspiracy theorists are not entirely sure, but most seem to accuse Bonds of experimenting with steroids before the 1999 season started. A few seem to think he started using steroids in 2000, just in time to hit 73 home runs in 2001. One thing we know for sure is that Bonds started using a Sam Bat in 1999. Before the 2001 season, when Bonds smashed the record 73 home runs, Holman created a special model Sam Bat—the 2K1—for Bonds. Bonds only broke one bat that whole season. They say he actually managed to hit a home run off the pitch that broke the bat. Whether that's true or not, Bonds was so satisfied with the Sam Bat's performance that he did something uncharacteristic—he treated Sam Holman and his employees with respect. Bonds traveled to Ottawa to publicly thank Holman. He toured the mill where Holman's people cut the maple. Bonds signed autographs and made a speech that partially credited Holman for the home-run record, noting that "it takes two to tango."

Theorizing that increased batting statistics may not be indicative of steroid use, baseball's leading statistical thinker, Bill James, says,

"I've never understood why nobody writes about it, but the bats are very different now than they were 20 years ago." He also notes that Barry Bonds's bats "are still different from everybody else's."

People who have already mentally convicted Bonds of steroid use won't want to give much thought to the Sam Bat. But a bat that adds five, 10, or 15 feet to the flight of the ball makes it awfully difficult to argue that Bonds must have been on steroids because he produced such great statistics after 1999. For those who desperately want to believe Bonds's home runs are steroid induced, it is probably best to forget about the Sam Bat altogether.

Something else happened after 1999. The Giants finally left Candlestick Park—gone with the wind, or at least, gone was the wind. While mornings at Candlestick were not all that bad, it was a cold, foggy, and windy place on summer evenings. The winds were legendary. In 1961, during the All-Star Game, pitcher Stu Miller (who won 14 games and saved 17 for the Giants that year) was literally blown off the mound. Well, maybe not literally blown off the mound, but the wind interfered with his delivery so much that he was called for a balk in the ninth inning. A couple of years later, the Mets were getting ready to start batting practice when a severe gust of wind hoisted the batting cage and blew it from behind home plate all the way to the pitcher's mound.

Candlestick, which was named after an odd-looking bird, was voted the worst major league ballpark by major league players in 1983. The New York Mets' All-Star first baseman, Keith Hernandez, actually negotiated a clause in his contract that barred the Mets from trading him to the Giants. Fans often arrived at Candlestick wearing gloves and ski jackets—in August. The Beatles played their last concert at Candlestick in 1966. The stage was behind second base, and John Lennon opened with an understatement, telling the crowd, "It's a bit chilly."

Willie Mays once said playing in Candlestick cost him 200 home runs. He would hit a shot, only to have the wind knock it down into the outfield. Mays was exaggerating, but there's little doubt that the extreme conditions made life more difficult for everyone who played at Candlestick. And the wind probably did cost Mays 30 or 40 home runs during the 12 years he played in the stadium by the Bay.

Beginning in 2000, Bonds and the Giants had a nice new stadium. The notorious wind that plagued Candlestick—wind that turned home runs into fly-ball outs—was gone. In its place was Pacific Bell Park, sporting a 309-foot right-field fence, as opposed to Candlestick's 328-foot right-field fence.

Even on the road, Bonds would now have a chance to play in ballparks that were more conducive to home runs than the ones they had replaced. Starting with the Baltimore Orioles' construction of Camden Yards, an accomplishment Larry Lucchino engineered in 1992, baseball saw an explosion of new (and hitter-friendly) stadiums. In 2000 a cozy Minute Maid Park replaced a cavernous Houston Astrodome. (Originally, Enron had paid more than $100 million for the naming rights, but the company ran into financial problems that were a little too difficult to resolve, and the Astros had to pay $2.1 million to get rid of the Enron name.) Coors Field in Denver went online in 1995. The Arizona Diamondbacks started playing at Chase Field (originally Bank One Ballpark) in 1998. In 2001 Pittsburgh's little PNC Park replaced a larger Three Rivers Stadium. And the list goes on. After the 1994 strike, the owners wanted offense. And the new stadiums seemed to be designed with that objective in mind.

Did the new stadiums really have an impact on the number of home runs? Schmidt thinks so:

> The proliferation of new ballparks over the past decade
> and a half, and their collective impact on baseball's records

and history, is quite another matter. They have had a huge impact. In the 20 seasons between 1973 (my first full year in the majors) and the opening of Camden Yards in 1992, the home-run rate was .65 per game. From 1993 through 2005, it was 1.04 per game.

According to Schmidt, today's National League hitters:

> get a crack at six "Wrigleys": Minute Maid in Houston, Miller Park in Milwaukee, Great American in Cincinnati, Bank One Ballpark in Phoenix, Citizens Bank in Philadelphia— and of course, good old Wrigley Field itself in Chicago. (Is the wind blowing out?) And then, as a special bonus for playing in the right era, they get to hit at Coors Field, every modern slugger's field of dreams.

The Polo Grounds and its 500-foot center-field fence is history. The hitter-friendly ballparks Bonds has regularly occupied since 2000 are a natural assist, especially for a left-handed hitter who was lifting weights to become more powerful, using a better bat, and waiting longer at the plate because of his protective equipment. And, as Bill Jenkinson reminds us, "[A]ll Major League stadiums now have backgrounds or so-called batting eyes in center field that aid the batter in seeing the ball as it's released from the pitcher's hand." A "batting eye" is a large area in center field with a dark background and no seats where, in the past, fans wearing white shirts would make it harder for batters to see the ball. Given all of these factors, should we have expected more home runs from Bonds even if he never touched a steroid? Absolutely! If Bonds had hit *fewer* home runs after 1999, *that* might have justified a federal investigation.

Something else happened in 1998—something else that made it harder to compare pre-1998 statistics with post-1998 statistics. The National League expanded by adding two teams. In 1997 there were 14 teams. In 1998, the Milwaukee Brewers and the Arizona Diamondbacks were added to the mix. (The Tampa Bay franchise was added to the American League and Milwaukee switched leagues.) The addition of two teams immediately diluted the available pitching talent. Overnight, the National League had 14 percent more pitchers. The addition of 20 to 30 pitchers who would have been toiling away in the minor leagues in 1997 might have made a bit of a difference. It was 1998, after all, when Sammy Sosa hit 66 home runs and Mark McGwire hit 70. (And let's not forget that the American League expanded from eight teams to 10 in 1961, the year Roger Maris hit 61 home runs.)

Undoubtedly, the presence of so many more marginal pitchers has made offensive production for the game's best hitters at least a little easier to achieve. Joe Morgan theorizes that the five-pitcher rotations that have been used universally since the early 1980s have also hurt the quality of pitching. Morgan reminds us that "20 percent of today's games are being started by pitchers who 20 years ago would have been middle relievers if they were fortunate enough to be on a major league roster at all. Too many clubs are rushing young pitchers to the majors to work as number-five starters."

Morgan wants to see a return to the four-pitcher rotation. He argues that pitching on three days' rest develops arm strength and improves control. While some (including Dr. Frank Jobe) worry that four-pitcher rotations would cause injuries, Morgan points to examples such as Warren Spahn, the Hall of Fame left-hander who typically started 39 or 40 games per season. As a 42-year-old, Spahn still had enough arm strength to pitch 259 innings and win 23 games against only seven losses (for a Milwaukee Braves team that finished sixth in the National League). Keith Woolner offers statistical support for Morgan's theory in *Five Starters or Four?: On Pitching and Stamina*. According to Woolner's statistics, pitching on three days' rest (as opposed to four) certainly did no harm to the pitcher's performance. It may have contributed to a slight improvement in performance.

Pitchers say there are other reasons for recent increases in offensive productivity. They emphasize the difficulties associated with pitching in the newly constructed hitter-friendly ballparks. And then they complain about video technology that allows hitters to closely study their motions. They even complain about the maple bats hitters are using. But far more important to the pitchers are two subtle changes the casual fan (and the steroid conspiracy theorist) might miss.

First, and most important, is the strike zone itself. Like your favorite T-shirt, the strike zone has shrunk over the years. People who are searching for an accurate description often characterize the current strike zone as about the size of a laptop computer. Those who are prone to exaggeration say it is about the size of a postage stamp.

Greg Maddux has pitched more than 4,700 innings, and he still hasn't walked 1,000 batters. In fact, subtract the intentional passes he's served up (more than 170), and Maddux hasn't even come close to walking 900. He is baseball's ultimate control pitcher, and, perhaps, along with Bonds, its most intelligent player. Even in 1998, when Sosa and McGwire were hitting all those home runs, Maddux posted a 2.22 earned-run average. But something happened in 1999: Maddux's ERA ballooned to 3.57. Umpires just weren't calling the close strikes the way they used to call them. As a result, Maddux noted, "Now you end up throwing...more pitches per inning. Multiply that...by 32 starts." In *Leo Mazzone's Tales from the Mound*, the Braves' unparalleled pitching coach discusses Maddux's practice routine. According to Mazzone, after every pitch Maddux would "always turn around...and say, 'That's a strike; that's a ball.'"

Suddenly, Mazzone was listening to Maddux turn around and say, "That used to be a strike."

Fewer close pitches were being called strikes. Batters had more pitches to choose from. Pitchers had to challenge hitters more often. Good hitters were hitting for higher averages, and they were hitting more home runs. Steroids were not causing umpires to call close pitches balls, were they?

One more subtle change was making life difficult for pitchers. Hitters no longer feared getting hit with the ball. In addition to the body armor, which made hitters more confident because they didn't have to worry so much about injuries, now a simple inside pitch would generate warnings to both teams. A pitcher that went inside again might get kicked out of the game. Hitters were able to dive over the plate to attack outside pitches like never before.

According to Yankees manager and former major league catcher Joe Torre, any hitter who had so aggressively attacked pitches on the outside corner a generation earlier would "get knocked on his ass, or at least have something to think about." In other words, "back in the day" pitchers threw the ball at batters who stood too close to the plate and attacked outside pitches. Hitters who wanted the best of both worlds would pay the price by risking their bodies.

Don Baylor was the American League's MVP in 1979, when he hit 36 home runs and drove in 139 runs for the California Angels. Baylor sees the new lack of hitter trepidation as the game's biggest change. According to Baylor, "All of the fear that used to be part of hitting has been taken away. Major League Baseball has taken away the aggressive side of this game. There is absolutely no fear factor."

The great Sandy Koufax described the importance of inside pitching this way: "Show me a pitcher who can't pitch inside, and I'll show you a loser." By 2000, there were very few pitchers who could effectively pitch inside. The fear that had restrained and contained prior generations of hitters—even the best hitters—was gone. Better protected by their equipment, the umpires, and the game's changing culture, batters suddenly had an extra split second to react. The extra time helped mediocre hitters, and it allowed supertalents like Barry Bonds to reach previously unattained levels.

*

It was April 16, 2004, and the Giants were hosting the Dodgers. The Dodgers took a 3–0 lead into the bottom of the ninth. To finish off the game, the Dodgers' manager, Jim Tracy, went to his Cy Young Award–winning closer, Eric Gagne. Officially, Gagne was listed at 6'2" and 195 pounds, but lately, he seemed bigger. In 2001 Gagne had struck out 130 batters in 151 innings. His ERA was 4.75. The next year, in 2002, Gagne was a completely different player. Now, he had a blazing fastball. His earned-run average was 1.97. He saved 52 games. He struck out 114 in just 82 innings. In 2003 Gagne won the Cy Young Award. He deserved it. He struck out 137 in just 82 innings, while walking only 20 batters. His ERA was an unbelievably low 1.20. He saved 55 games.

The 42,662 fans who attended that Giants-Dodgers game on April 16, 2004, were in for a treat—that is, if they stuck around long enough to see the last inning. With a runner on and one out in the bottom of the ninth, Bonds came to the plate. Gagne fired three quick fastballs, breaking the 100 mph barrier. Bonds just watched. And then Bonds watched a tantalizingly slow curveball fall outside the strike zone. The count was 2–2. The rest of the Giants were glad they were watching instead of trying to hit off Gagne. Bonds's teammates recalled Gagne's "nasty, nasty, unhittable stuff that nobody can touch."

Two more 100 mph fastballs were fouled off. Then Gagne let go—a 101 mph fastball that rocketed toward the inside corner of the plate. Bonds stepped forward and delivered his usual smooth but powerful swing. He connected. The ball was launched over the center-field fence for a two-run home run. A witness, Bonds's teammate Dustin Mohr, said, "I saw that and thought, 'I'll never be able to do that.' Never, ever, ever. It was a home run only the most gifted among us could hit."

After he retired the side to record the save, Gagne said, "That's why he's the greatest player ever. I have a lot of respect for him; I respected him, and he killed it."

Bonds can handle the heat. During the 2002 World Series, Bonds faced off against Troy Percival, the Angels closer—a closer who finished the season with 40 saves and a 1.92 earned-run average. Percival was a strikeout artist who could bring the ball to the plate at speeds approaching 100 mph. In the second game, with the Angels leading 11–9 and no runners on base, Percival went right after Bonds. Bonds crushed a 97 mph fastball. The home run landed in a tunnel in the bleachers, some 485 feet from home plate. TV cameras caught Tim Salmon in the Angels' dugout visibly mouthing the words, "That's the farthest ball I've ever seen."

The odd thing is that the faster a ball is pitched, the more distance the ball will travel when the bat hits it. So, as the strike zone shrank, and as batters were allowed to wear armor, crowd the plate, and use harder yet lighter bats—all while knowing excessive inside pitching would result in the pitcher being warned or tossed from the game, there may have been a few pitchers who wanted to try to find a way to reduce the hitters' advantage, a way to make the proverbial playing field just a little more even.

Take Jason Grimsley, a journeyman relief pitcher (and occasional starter) who toiled in the major leagues from 1989 to 2006. Grimsley won 42 games and lost 58. His career earned-run average was 4.77. Grimsley was pitching for the Arizona Diamondbacks in June 2006, but his career was almost over. Apparently, Grimsley confessed on April 19, 2006, and told federal agents he had used banned or illegal drugs during his career. Of course, Grimsley had tested positive for steroids when baseball first implemented testing in 2003. Grimsley told agents about amphetamines, and he said that he switched to human growth hormone after he tested positive for steroids. In June, federal agents raided Grimsley's home. The confession became public, and Grimsley's pitching career ended.

Grimsley wasn't the only pitcher who used steroids. During 2005, 65 minor league players and 11 major league players were suspended for using steroids or other banned, performance-enhancing drugs. Of those 76 players, almost 50 percent were pitchers. Thirty-six pitchers were suspended for using steroids. Maybe steroids can add a few more miles per hour to the fastball. Maybe that's why it seems like every other pitcher in the major leagues now throws in the mid- to high 90s. But hitters like Bonds eat fast, straight pitches for lunch. The extra speed just means the ball goes that much farther when he connects. So, ironically, mediocre pitchers who are taking steroids and adding a few extra miles per hour to their fastball could be a factor that is contributing to the significant home-run totals the game's greatest sluggers are now amassing.

Jenkinson is a dedicated baseball historian. His recent and very entertaining book is called *The Year Babe Ruth Hit 104 Home Runs: Recrowning Baseball's Greatest Slugger*. Jenkinson has a bit of a bias toward Ruth, and he can't help but show it. Jenkinson's painstaking research led him to conclude that home-run distance measures show that Bonds used steroids. Jenkinson's theory goes something like this: he believes most real power hitters "peaked for distance" at age 27 or 28. Jenkinson says Bonds peaked at or after age 36. Therefore, according to Jenkinson, "Barry Bonds has almost certainly used steroids to achieve what he has achieved."

The problems with Jenkinson's attack on Bonds are many and fairly obvious. Let's start with the difficulty in obtaining precise measurements of home runs. Home-run distance cannot always be measured. For example, some people believe Mantle hit a home run that would have traveled more than 700 feet. Mantle hit the prodigious shot in 1963, when he was 31 years old (several years after Jenkinson believes most hitters "peak for distance"). No one really has any idea how far the ball would have traveled because it hit part of the stadium a mere 370 feet from home plate. You can use a mathematical formula to try to estimate the distance of such a hit, but a formula is only as accurate as the assumptions that are used to feed the formula. Was the ball rising when it made contact with the stadium? Or was it already descending? What was the ball's angle of travel or trajectory? How fast was the ball traveling? Was there a tail wind at that moment? A wind swirl? And so on.

Similarly, the estimated distance of Mantle's 565-foot Griffith Stadium home run (which, incidentally, was hit when Mantle was just 21 years old), depends on the purported eyewitness testimony of Donald Dunaway. Unfortunately, Dunaway was only 10 years old in 1953. Adding to the problem is the fact that the New York Yankees' public relations director, Red Patterson, paced the distance off and estimated. He did not use a tape measure. But it gets worse. The ball hit a beer sign in midflight and then ricocheted. No one will ever really know how far the ball would have traveled absent the obstruction.

There just is no sure way to measure the distance of many home runs. The farther the ball travels, the harder it is to accurately measure distance. So, Jenkinson's theory rests on a series of estimates—often the estimates of people who have an interest in exaggerating. In *The Physics of Baseball*, Dr. Robert Adair refers to such an estimate as an "uninformed wild guess."

The questionable nature of Jenkinson's data is not the only problem with his theory. Jenkinson uses home-run distance as a proxy for strength and strength as a proxy for steroid use. Anyone who has seen Michelle Wie hit a golf ball knows Jenkinson has managed to confuse himself in the worst possible way. Wie is a teenage girl. She is lanky and relatively thin—not exactly a buffed-out weight lifter. In 2004, when she was all of 15 years old, Wie's average golf drive was more than 270 yards. Wie can hit a golf ball far because of her swing mechanics and rotational capabilities, not because she has powerful muscles. And not because she uses steroids.

A golf ball just sits there waiting to be hit. Compared to baseball, golf has fewer distance-related variables. Swing, club, tee, ball, and wind are pretty much all there is. There is no Joel Zumaya throwing 101 mph fastballs. Remember, if other factors are held steady, the faster the pitch, the less strength it takes to drive it a great distance. At first, this seems counterintuitive. However, we don't need a physics degree to understand the principle. Think about it this way—imagine a baseball sitting on a tee. You square off to bunt and lightly push the ball forward with the bat. The ball dribbles off the tee and rolls about two or three feet forward. Now, imagine a Zumaya fastball. Even if Zumaya's arm is a little sore from playing too much Guitar Hero (the world's best, and probably most addictive, video game), when the batter squares off to bunt, he actually pulls the bat backward to try to deaden the ball as the bat and ball connect. The ball still shoots down the third-base line. The energy of the pitch was reversed, and the speed Zumaya imparted to his fastball was turned into distance that wouldn't exist if a stationary ball was bunted off the tee.

Still other variables confound Jenkinson's theory. Everything from the quality of the bat to the weight and hardness of the baseball can make a difference in the distance a home run travels. While swing mechanics can be more important than strength, Jenkinson cannot account for one other factor—and it is a big one. The overwhelming majority of the players Jenkinson studied did not start an intense weight-lifting program midway through their professional careers. Bonds did. Weightlifting creates strength, whether it is combined with steroids or not. So, whatever contribution strength makes to the distance a ball travels, the conclusion Jenkinson draws from his study would be erroneous. Jenkinson has no way to measure strength increases resulting from lifting weights as opposed to strength increases that result from steroid use.

Jenkinson also does not account for changes in (or refinements to) a player's swing. Different swings can create different ball trajectories, and a baseball's trajectory is a significant factor in the distance the ball will travel off the bat. Bonds made changes to his swing that improved his trajectory. Describing Bonds in 2001, his teammate Eric Davis noted that Bonds's "trajectory is just outstanding." Davis went on to point out that Bonds was "getting the ball in the air" with greater frequency. Better trajectory meant more home runs and longer home runs. Kiner hit 54 home runs for the Pirates in 1949. Watching Bonds hit 73 home runs in 2001, Kiner said, "There is nothing about his swing to criticize. It is one of the greatest swings I've ever seen." Steroids do not improve the quality of a player's swing or his ability to generate trajectory that maximizes distance.

In 2001 Jenkinson said Ruth would have hit 84 home runs in 1927 if the Babe had played his games in homer-friendly modern ballparks. By the time Jenkinson's book hit the shelves in 2007, the Babe was up to 91 home runs in 1927 and 104 in 1921. After Bonds suggested that he might be able to eclipse some of Ruth's records, Jenkinson's research was used to fuel the attacks against Bonds. Jenkinson's research doesn't show that Bonds (or anyone else) used steroids, but Jenkinson did prove that he knew how to generate some buzz for his easy-to-read and entertaining book.

Ultimately, statistics prove Bonds was good, not that he used steroids.

Testimonials

The last major part of the case against Bonds consists of what people have said about him—people like Kimberly Bell, Jeff Novitzky, Victor Conte, Greg Anderson, and Barry Bonds himself. Unless you hate Bonds and have already decided that he used steroids, you will want to evaluate the context of the statements that have been made against him. What is the motivation of the person who is doing the talking? How credible is that person? Is there a bias?

California's Evidence Code tells us to evaluate a witness based on his or her "demeanor while testifying" and "the existence or nonexistence of a bias, interest, or other motive." People who are fair-minded and want to carefully assess the testimony that has helped to convict Bonds in the court of public opinion will not have the benefit of watching witnesses testify in a courtroom. So we really can't evaluate demeanor, such as hesitation, shifty eyes, or reading off a script, that would allow a jury to gauge a witness's credibility. But we can still evaluate the bias, interest, or other motive of each person who has something to say about whether or not Bonds used steroids.

Some people are convinced that the Internal Revenue Service's BALCO raid produced powerful evidence that Bonds used steroids. Did it? To answer that question we need to take another look at the information the raid produced and to evaluate the interests, bias, and motivations of the participants.

Let's start with BALCO's president, the "mad scientist" and "egomaniac" Conte. During the infamous September 3, 2003, BALCO raid, IRS agent Novitzky took Conte to a conference room. Novitzky says Conte voluntarily spoke to him for more than three hours. Novitzky says Conte explained his distribution of the Clear and the Cream and implicated 27 athletes. One of the implicated athletes—according to Novitzky—was Bonds. Novitzky says Conte told him Anderson had brought in several baseball players before the start of the 2003 season (which was to be the first season with Major League Baseball steroid testing in place). Conte supposedly told Novitzky BALCO had supplied Bonds with the Clear and the Cream and that Bonds used those substances "on a regular basis."

Who was Conte? What were his motivations? And what did he really say about Bonds? Let's start by acknowledging the obvious—Conte has called *Game of Shadows* "full of outright lies." He sees the book as "character assassination of Barry Bonds and myself." There is, of course, no doubt that its authors, Lance Williams and Mark Fainaru-Wada, don't like Conte or Bonds. And their book does repeatedly attack the people, rather than the problem. Yet, *Shadows* itself contains substantial information that undermines the accusation that Conte can offer any evidence as to whether Bonds used steroids.

Shadows paints a picture of Conte as a lowlife who happened to have something of a photographic memory, slightly unusual musical talent, and usually, substantially more intelligence than those who were around him. The *Shadows* authors say Conte was a good enough bass player to join Tower of Power. His cousin, Bruce Conte, played guitar and sang background for Tower of Power, and Victor is credited on the band's 1978 album, *We Came to Play*. But the book implies that Conte was not exceptionally talented and "got the job basically because he was Bruce's cousin." *Shadows* tells us Victor was kicked out of the band after he tried to take control over the whole operation.

But "even amidst the drugged-out world of TOP," *Shadows* says, "Conte had worked out with weights and taken vitamin pills, preaching a spiritually healthy existence." Together with his wife,

Conte opened the Millbrae Holistic Health Center. And soon, Conte was obsessed with the nutrition business. According to *Shadows*, this represented "an improbable conversion, but Conte possessed a reptilian facility for changing his skin. He viewed whatever business he chose as merely a forum for his rise to greatness." From *Shadows* we learn that Conte was desperate for fame and fortune but that he "wasn't the kind of person who was good at keeping secrets."

Shadows tells us Conte was giving erythropoietin (EPO, the endurance drug), human growth hormone, and the Clear to track stars such as Marion Jones and Tim Montgomery. Ironically, Montgomery was supposedly using so many steroids before he hooked up with Conte that Conte told him he would need to cut back on his steroid intake.

Conte had two attributes that created problems for the athletes he "tutored." First, he really wanted credit for the success his athletes achieved. Second, Conte had a big mouth. (Maybe that's two facets of a single problem.) When Conte had a falling-out with Montgomery, he vowed to "create a sprinter even better than Montgomery." Conte tended to see himself as more important than the athletes he assisted. It stands to reason that *if* Conte was supplying the Clear, HGH, or other performance-enhancing substances to Bonds, Conte would want to take at least partial credit for Bonds's unprecedented success. Bonds, after all, did hit 73 home runs in 2001, and he was widely recognized as among baseball's top-five players of all time. Even though Bonds was no track star, he was a big name in a big sport. It would have been out of character for Conte to keep quiet if there was any way he could claim responsibility for Bonds's greatness.

The IRS agent who set out to get Bonds, Novitzky, says Conte did brag about being responsible for all those home runs Bonds hit. On September 5, 2003, Novitzky prepared a memorandum detailing the IRS BALCO raid that had occurred two days earlier. Paragraph eight of Novitzky's memo says, "Conte has given 'the Clear' and 'the

Cream' and advised on its use to the following professional athletes in the following sports." That paragraph goes on to list Barry Bonds under the heading "MLB." Paragraph 22 of Novitzky's memo, near the end of the document, says, "Bonds does not pay Conte for 'Clear' and 'the Cream' that he receives. Bonds's payment is in the form of promotion for Conte's ZMA product."

Should we believe Novitzky? There are at least a few reasons to be skeptical. Why was the memo prepared on Friday? The raid took place on September 3, 2003—a Wednesday. What did Novitzky do on Thursday, September 4, 2003, that was so important? Why did that memo have to wait? And, far more important, why didn't Novitzky have a tape recorder at the raid? If Novitzky had a tape recorder, the whole world ultimately could have heard Conte's statements and we all could have judged for ourselves. The BALCO/Bonds investigation had become Novitzky's life. He had spent many evenings sifting through BALCO trash. Novitzky *carefully* prepared for the raid. He brought along 25 agents and experts in important subjects. He even brought a photographer. Why, and how, could he possibly not have brought a tape recorder?

Although Conte subsequently questioned the voluntariness of the Novitzky interview, claiming that Novitzky held him at gunpoint and never told Conte about his Miranda rights, Novitzky says the interview was 100 percent voluntary. So, according to the IRS criminal investigation procedure manual, Novitzky had options. He could have used a qualified stenographer to record and transcribe the interview, the same way a court reporter would make a record of questions and answers during a deposition or during court testimony. Alternatively, Novitzky could have used a simple tape recorder. Instead, by waiting a couple of days and then typing up a short memo summarizing the lengthy interview, Novitzky left us all to wonder exactly what Conte really said.

Novitzky says Conte was cooperative, if not anxious to brag about his exploits. If so, why not record the interview? Even if Novitzky forgot a tape recorder, he could have easily called for one. At the very least, Novitzky could have prepared a short, written statement confirming Conte's purported confession, and allowed Conte to sign it under penalty of perjury. Instead, Novitzky left us with no detailed or accurate record of Conte's statements, and no contemporaneous record of Conte's alleged direct condemnation of Bonds.

To decide who might be telling the truth, it might be helpful to assess motivation. What incentive, if any, did Conte have to lie? And what incentive, if any, did Novitzky have to embellish?

Conte had no reason to protect Barry Bonds. Bonds was not paying money to Conte. Bonds was a superstar in a major sport—a superstar who had just broken baseball's most notable single-season record and was amassing statistics that would arguably make him baseball's greatest all-time slugger. If Conte was ready to confess to the IRS, and if he was even half of the egomaniac we have heard about, and if he really did give steroids to Bonds and coach him on their proper use, there was no reason for Conte to hold back—no reason for Conte to protect Bonds.

With respect to many other athletes, Conte *supports* Novitzky's recollection as documented by the memorandum Novitzky prepared on September 5, 2003. A year after the raid, Conte agreed to an interview for the television program *20/20*, and he didn't hesitate to finger those athletes he had assisted with steroids, performance-enhancing drugs, and related "coaching." For example, on national television Conte calmly explained that he gave Marion Jones the Clear, EPO, HGH, and insulin. And Conte was detailed. He described personally observing Jones injecting performance-enhancing drugs. Conte told us she preferred to inject the front part of her leg, as opposed to her stomach area.

In terms of being a famous athlete, Jones was certainly in the same universe as Bonds, if not the same league. She had won five medals in the 2000 Olympic Games in Sydney, Australia. She was widely regarded as the fastest woman on Earth. And even initially, Conte's accusations had some degree of credibility, particularly since Jones's "A" sample tested positive for synthetic EPO in mid-2006, after she won the 100 meters event at the U.S. Track and Field championships in Indianapolis. (Jones's "B" sample subsequently tested clean, at least temporarily exonerating her.) During his 2004 *20/20* interview, Conte predicted that it would be difficult to catch Jones red-handed. He explained that accurate drug tests to detect the substances Jones used did not exist. According to Conte, beating the drug tests was "like taking candy from a baby." Jones vehemently denied Conte's statements. All that changed in early April 2007, when a shocked world heard that Jones admitted taking the Clear and elected to plead guilty to charges of lying to a federal agent. Jones says she received the Clear from her coach, Trevor Graham, beginning in 1999. Jones's belated admission seems to enhance Conte's credibility.

During the interview, Conte implicated other athletes as well. He bragged about the regimen he prepared for sprinter Kelli White, calling it "the most sophisticated in the history of the planet Earth." Unlike Jones, White acknowledges using the substances Conte provided. Unlike Jones, White credits Conte's creations for helping her win gold medals in the 100- and 200-meter events at the 2003 world championships in Paris. Similarly, Conte boasted of his secret plan to turn Montgomery into the world's fastest man, and he acknowledged giving steroids to Bill Romanowski and other professional football players.

But Conte refused, and continues to refuse, to say that he gave steroids to Bonds. Conte says he has "never given anabolic steroids or any other performance enhancing drug to Barry Bonds." Conte goes even further, saying he has "never had a discussion about anabolic steroids with Barry Bonds, and that's the truth." If Conte gave Bonds steroids, why lie about it now? Why lie about it in 2003? Conte seems to have nothing to gain by lying. Did he really think Bonds was going to be BALCO's spokesperson? More important, Conte has never been the type of person to hold back. When he was released from prison in March 2006, Conte told reporters prison was like a men's retreat. Conte bragged that he was able to read, give music lessons to other inmates, coach a running team, and engage in steroid debates. Conte, like the rest of us, has faults. But shyness isn't one of them. If he gave Bonds steroids, he would probably tell us. Heck, he would probably say something like, "I worked up a program for Bonds that was more advanced than any steroid program in the history of our solar system, whether Pluto counts as a planet or not."

Interestingly enough, the *Shadows* authors claim to have inside information about what Conte told attorneys shortly after the September 3, 2003, BALCO raid. For example, *Shadows* tells us that Conte bragged to attorney Troy Ellerman, telling Ellerman that he had supplied performance-enhancing drugs to Bonds. *Shadows'* source notes credit "two sources with knowledge of their interactions," sources who allegedly revealed the discussions between Conte and the attorney. But California's Professional Responsibility Rules make attorney-client communications confidential. And California's Evidence Code makes attorney-client communications privileged. Even if Conte never officially hired Ellerman (who actually ended up representing BALCO vice president Jim Valente), their discussions were still confidential and probably protected by the privilege. Absent Conte's permission, disclosure appears highly inappropriate. But this is what makes speculation by unnamed sources about what a client told an attorney an ideal way to attack in the court of public opinion.

Then there's the Ellerman problem. Ellerman may have been using Fainaru-Wada and Williams to help him fabricate a defense for his ultimate client, Jim Valente. Did Ellerman really give the reporters information that was supposed to be kept secret so that he could cry foul when the reporters leaked the information to the public? The whole thing sounds incredibly preposterous. Yet, it looks like that's exactly what happened. Ellerman leaked grand jury transcripts to Fainaru-Wada. The Shadows authors made a name for themselves by using the leaked grand jury testimony Ellerman shouldn't have shared with them. Then the journalists kept quiet as Ellerman blamed the government for the leaks and asked the court to dismiss the case because the government leaks prevented his client from getting a fair trial. Ellerman ultimately admitted the improper disclosure of grand jury testimony, pled guilty, and was sentenced to 2½ years in prison. He resigned his California State Bar membership in 2007. His wrongdoing was extreme and shocking. And it put the two *Chronicle* journalists in an awkward position. Although District Judge Susan Illston was not persuaded by Ellerman's fabricated argument (and she denied the motion to dismiss on December 28, 2004), there was a period of time where the reporters must have known their silence might even give Conte and Valente a chance to avoid prosecution. The journalists apparently decided that their access to information was more important than anything else. But their decision couldn't have been easy.

Because there is not much reliable evidence to the contrary, we need to acknowledge one possibility. Maybe, just maybe, Novitzky made up the part about Conte acknowledged giving steroids and HGH to Bonds. But I don't think so. Of course it is possible that Novitzky's September 5, 2003, memo is a pure fabrication when it comes to Bonds. That is what Conte seems to think. But the far more likely explanation is that Novitzky just got it wrong. Undoubtedly, Novitzky wanted to nail Bonds in the worst possible way. So regardless of what Conte actually said about Bonds, Novitzky probably heard what he wanted to hear—no more and no less. Then, two days later, Novitzky typed up a memo that inadvertently put words in Conte's mouth—words Conte never said, but words Novitzky was hoping to hear.

Why was Novitzky inclined to prejudge the evidence? Why was he willing to spend night after night knee deep in BALCO's trash? Maybe Novitzky wanted to protect boyhood idols, like Hank Aaron. At about the time the BALCO indictments were handed down, Attorney General John Ashcroft supposedly told aides, "Stan Musial didn't need steroids. Let me tell you something. Back before they were allowed to wear body armor, if some guy was known to be taking drugs like that, you can bet Bob Gibson would give them some chin music."

Meanwhile, Ashcroft's director of public affairs, Mark Corallo, explained the indictments by saying:

> This really wasn't about BALCO. In the end, it had nothing to do with Victor Conte and Greg Anderson and their activity. It had to do with the guys who had been cheating Stan Musial and Mickey Mantle and Lou Gehrig and Hank Aaron and Willie Mays; that's what this was about. That's who they are cheating; they're cheating the baseball immortals, and they're cheating the fans. And it means something.

Maybe Novitzky saw Mark McGwire, Roger Maris, Hank Aaron, or even Babe Ruth, as the "real" home-run king. Or maybe Novitzky was just like so many other sports fans—fed up with the way Bonds treated people. That's how Iran White sees it. White worked for the California Bureau of Narcotics Enforcement. White had a history of working with Novitzky. Novitzky asked him to work on the BALCO case.

As part of a multiagency investigation under the supervision of attorney Jeffrey Nedrow (the same attorney who would question

Bonds before the grand jury at the end of 2003), Novitzky put the muscular White deep undercover. White infiltrated the Bay Area Fitness where Anderson—Bonds's personal trainer—worked with his regular customers. Anderson soon had White, a former sprinter who was now a muscular 46-year-old, as a regular customer. White wore a concealed recording device. The regular workouts with Anderson revealed that Anderson was extremely proud—actually, a little boastful—of his relationship with Bonds. But the weeks went by without Anderson (1) offering White steroids, or (2) telling White that he gave or sold Bonds steroids. In other words, just as the San Mateo County sheriff's undercover probe a few years earlier had failed to produce any evidence suggesting that Anderson was a steroid supplier for Bonds (or anyone else), Novitzky and White also came up empty.

In May 2003, after a particularly grueling workout with Anderson, White went home and, unfortunately, suffered a stroke. With that, government efforts to record Anderson saying something about giving or selling steroids to Bonds came to an end. Nevertheless, perhaps more than any other person, White had been in a position to know exactly what was driving Novitzky. Why would Novitzky spend his evenings sifting through BALCO's trash just to see if he could find a single piece of paper implicating Bonds? According to White, the answer was simple. And it was exactly what we should have expected. During a casual conversation between White and Novitzky, Novitzky revealed his motivation. Novitzky told White that Bonds was "a great athlete." And then Novitzky asked, "Do you think he's on steroids?" White hesitated, then said, "They're all on steroids—all of our top major leaguers."

But that wasn't good enough for Novitzky. He wasn't worried about all major leaguers. Novitzky was worried about Bonds. Novitzky calmly told White he'd "sure like to prove" Bonds was on steroids because Bonds is "such an asshole to the press." So, the easiest explanation is also the most likely. Like so many others, Novitzky could not stand the way Bonds treated people. Unlike so many others, Novitzky was in a position to do something about it. And he dedicated a lot of his energy to getting Bonds. To some people, that makes Novitzky a hero. However, Novitzky may have had a little too much enthusiasm. One night after a hard workout with Anderson, White hooked up with Novitzky. White said Novitzky was talking about a possible book deal, and he was absolutely jubilant over the June 2003 publication of *Muscle and Fitness*—a magazine that featured a piece on Bonds, the training he received from Anderson, and the purported nutritional value of Conte's ZMA product. Although this "article" was nothing more than a glossy ad for Conte's ZMA, White says Novitzky was ecstatic as he told White, "Buy some drugs from that f*cker, and I'll buy you a steak."

Novitzky was probably not intentionally lying when he prepared his memorandum detailing his discussions with Conte. But it also seems unlikely that Conte told Novitzky he gave Bonds steroids or told Bonds how to use steroids. If anything, Conte gave steroids and steroid coaching to Anderson—not to Bonds. And Bonds took a few minutes to pose for some photos that would help Conte sell some ZMA. Novitzky's memorandum is probably flawed. But the flaw does not reflect a purposeful fabrication. Instead, Novitzky was overly excited during the interview. When Conte talked, Novitzky's mind was racing. And two days later, Novitzky typed what he *thought* he had heard rather than what Conte had actually said.

If the discussion had been tape-recorded we would not have heard Conte say he gave steroids to Bonds. Victor Conte never gave steroids to Bonds. He never watched Bonds inject steroids or ingest steroids. Conte just is not in a position to tell us whether or not Barry Bonds used steroids. And neither is Novitzky. If Bonds used steroids, Novitzky was doing the Lord's work in revealing it. But, no matter how well intentioned he may have been, his personal investment in the outcome raises serious questions. When a law enforcement officer personally invests himself in one particular and predetermined outcome of an investigation, bad things can happen—whether a book deal is in the works or not.

*

Even if Conte wasn't in a position to finger Bonds for steroid use, Anderson certainly was. Anderson spent many hours with Bonds, encouraging him to push harder, to lift weights with more intensity, to do more reps, to use heavier weights, and so on. Anderson had access to Bonds in the Giants' clubhouse. Many people have assumed without hesitation that Anderson provided steroids and HGH for Bonds, taught Bonds to use them, and helped Bonds conceal his use from others. But is there any actual proof that Anderson gave steroids to Bonds?

We know that at least two different undercover operations failed to generate a single statement connecting Anderson and Bonds with respect to steroids. Anderson certainly profited from his relationship with Bonds. It helped him get clients. He also profited from selling steroids, or so we are told. Yet, even with government agents wearing hidden recording devices while Anderson tried to sell his services, not a single Anderson statement links Bonds and steroids. Undercover agents apparently couldn't even get Anderson to offer steroids to them. Maybe Anderson (whom Williams and Fainaru-Wada describe as a tattooed gym rat) was just too smart. Maybe he was too cautious and too careful to slip up even once. Maybe he was too clever to be fooled by experienced law enforcement officials.

When Novitzky finally got his turn with Anderson on the evening of September 3, 2003, there was still nothing to link Bonds and steroids. According to Novitzky's memo, federal agents met Anderson at the Bay Area Fitness, where he was working with clients. They told

Anderson they had a search warrant for his home and car. Novitzky drove Anderson and his young son to Anderson's apartment. A "voluntary" interview ensued. Anderson said he primarily provided steroids for bodybuilders. However, he did acknowledge that he had given some athletes steroids and human growth hormone. When professional baseball implemented steroid testing at the major league level, Anderson paid cash to obtain the Clear and the Cream from BALCO (primarily from its vice president, Valente).

During the interview, Novitzky pressed Anderson to name names. Anderson did. He told Novitzky he had given HGH to Benito Santiago and Bobby Estalella. Anderson said he helped to train the British sprinter Dwain Chambers but did not give Chambers steroids. And finally, when asked point-blank about Bonds, Anderson said Bonds never used the Cream or the Clear.

There seem to be at least two reasons why Anderson had every incentive to rat out Bonds, *if* Bonds used steroids. First, if Anderson really wanted to look like a steroid expert, tying Bonds to steroids would have allowed him to take credit for the single-season home-run record and all of Bonds's other recent exploits. Second, and perhaps more important, Anderson almost certainly could have avoided jail time if he agreed to testify against Bonds. Instead, Anderson elected to plead guilty to steroid distribution and money laundering, and he spent several months in jail. Then, when Anderson refused to testify before a grand jury, he was forced to spend a lot more time in jail on contempt charges. Anderson believed the deal he struck when he agreed to plead guilty in 2005 prevented him from being forced to testify before the grand jury, and his attorneys argued that the grand jury proceedings were tainted because illegally obtained evidence had been used.

You might assume Bonds treated Anderson like royalty because of everything Anderson had done for him. But you would be wrong. Bonds rarely paid Anderson, and the sporadic payments were never particularly large. Bonds regularly belittled and humiliated Anderson, to the point that Anderson tried to avoid speaking to other people whenever Bonds was nearby. Talking to anyone other than Bonds too often led to verbal tirades Anderson wanted to avoid. This type of treatment gave Anderson a bit of "get even" motivation to say he had seen Bonds use steroids.

With the federal government still out to get Bonds for perjury or tax evasion, there may come a time when Anderson decides that his self-interest requires him to testify that he gave steroids to Bonds. Unfortunately, any such new and contradictory testimony will not be particularly convincing because of the circumstances that led to the testimony. People who care about the truth will be forced to confront the fact that Anderson did not implicate Bonds when he was being secretly recorded by government agents. People who care about the truth will be forced to confront the fact that Anderson initially told Novitzky he did *not* give steroids to Bonds.

But what about the secret recording the *Shadows* authors obtained? Remember that former athlete (who does not want his identity revealed) who struck up a conversation with Anderson when Anderson didn't know he was being recorded? The nine-minute, 19-second recording had Anderson talking about problems that can confront inexperienced steroid users. And the tape has Anderson bragging about his inside knowledge of baseball's steroid-testing program. Just as Anderson may have exaggerated his relationship with Bonds, it seems he also exaggerated his knowledge of baseball's steroid-testing program. According to Major League Baseball's Rob Manfred, an executive vice president in charge of steroid testing, there was just no way Anderson or anyone else could have known a week or two in advance that Bonds or any other player would be tested.

In fact, Anderson even exaggerated his knowledge of steroids. In the secret recording Anderson blames the location of injections for the inevitable infections:

What happens is, they put too much in one area, and what it does, it will actually ball up and puddle, and what happens is, it will eat away and make an indentation, and it's a cyst. It makes a big f*cking cyst, and you have to drain it. Oh, no, it's gnarly.

No, dude, you'd be amazed at how many bodybuilders— 'cause bodybuilders do like f*ck*ing sometimes 20 CCs of shit, and it's just ugly…. It gets infected, I mean, they got to drain—I've had a guy had two gallons of shit drained out of his ass. It was so gross, you can't even believe it.

People don't know what the f*ck they're doing, that's the problem. No, I've seen all kinds of ugly shit, it's just unbelievable…. I learned that when I first started doing that shit 16 years ago 'cause guys were getting some gnarly infections. And it was gross, I mean to the point we have to have surgery just to get that f*cking thing taken out, or it'd be a knot and you can't do anything. That's why you never do your quad. Dude, I never, never. I tell you, I knew a guy that went in their own quad, and they went too deep and they couldn't walk for a week, could not even bend their leg. It was some ugly shit.

Anderson didn't know what he was talking about. It isn't needle-insertion location that causes infection. Dirty needles cause infections. Harrison Pope is a doctor who teaches at Harvard Medical School. Pope gives us a reason to laugh at Anderson's lack of basic knowledge. According to Pope:

They're not using clean needles, and of course you get infections. Unless the needle is sterile, bacteria is introduced deep into the steroid user's muscle, and as the infection takes hold, a pus-filled cyst called an abscess is formed. I've seen 20 or 30 guys who have experienced an abscess, and it's been the result of a dirty needle.

Most of us would take Pope's word on this subject over Anderson's. But maybe the federal government sees it differently. In his September 8, 2003, memo Novitzky says Anderson "displayed an above-average knowledge of anabolic steroids and their properties." Well, Anderson's knowledge certainly wasn't above average for steroid experts. Was it above average for personal trainers? Or was Novitzky just noting that as compared to most people, Anderson knew a lot about steroids? In reality, it looks like Anderson tried to convey the impression that he knew a lot of things he really did not know. He was no steroid guru. He was a weight guru who was marketing his services as a personal trainer and doing a little puffing about steroids.

On the secret tape, Anderson also discussed Bonds, saying he "thinks the magic's gone, [that] he doesn't have it anymore."

The parts of the secret tape the *Shadows* authors are willing to quote do not actually have Anderson saying that Bonds used steroids, or even that Anderson gave him steroids. Nevertheless, the *Shadows* authors say this secret recording reveals that Anderson claimed "Barry Bonds was using an 'undetectable' performance-enhancing drug during the 2003 baseball season."

Another question we have to ask is, does the tape have evidentiary value? Maybe, but not much. Anderson's attorneys insist the tape is so poor in quality that it isn't possible to confirm that it is actually Anderson's voice on the tape. There seems to be no direct statement on the tape where Anderson says he gave Bonds steroids. The tape seems to be nothing more than statements that were not made in court and not made under oath. As a result, even if the tape included direct incriminating statements against Bonds, its usefulness in a case against Bonds is not readily apparent.

There is one other problem with the tape. Like some of the other "evidence" *Shadows* discusses, it may have been obtained inappropriately, if not illegally. California law prohibits eavesdropping. Penal Code section 632 provides for imprisonment and fines for a person who "intentionally and without the consent of all parties to a confidential communication, by means of any electronic amplifying recording device eavesdrops upon or records the confidential communication ..." If a private conversation was recorded without Anderson's knowledge and permission, there is a good chance the tape recording was illegally obtained. If so, this is one more reason to question the tape's evidentiary value.

But what about Valente, BALCO's vice president? Maybe he gave steroids to Bonds. Perhaps the unassuming Valente can offer the key piece of evidence, the convincing proof that Bonds broke home-run records because of a bodily transformation that resulted from incessant steroid use. Valente seems to be everything Conte was not. He is quiet and content to play the role of loyal underling. Valente also spoke to Novitzky during the BALCO raid. Novitzky says Valente told him "Bonds has received 'the Clear' and 'the Cream' from BALCO on a 'couple of occasions.'" Novitzky's slightly belated memorandum, prepared five days after Novitzky and Valente spoke, says, "Bonds does not like how 'the Clear' makes him feel." It seems just a little strange that Valente also told Novitzky he had personally tried the Clear, but "did not like how it made him feel."

Although this was the most important investigation of Novitzky's life—an investigation that would quickly lead to the U.S. attorney general, Ashcroft, announcing indictments on national TV—there was no recording. And Valente recalls a different conversation.

Aside from the almost unbelievable failure to record these incredibly significant conversations, there is another evidentiary problem with the memo Novitzky prepared. There is almost no detail. The memorandum leaves us asking several questions:

1. How did Valente know Bonds had tried the Clear?
2. Did Valente personally observe Bonds ingesting the Clear?
3. When and where did Bonds use the Clear? Was he at Valente's house? Was he at BALCO? Did Valente visit Bonds at Bonds's house? At Pac Bell Park?
4. What exactly did Bonds tell Valente about the Clear? What were his exact words?

The lack of specificity about Bonds is particularly glaring because Novitzky's memo casually mentions that "Valente was physically present in a room when Conte was explaining and distributing 'the Clear' and 'Cream' to Bill Romanowski of the Oakland Raiders." There are no similar statements to reveal how Valente learned that Bonds had used the Clear and the Cream on a "couple of occasions."

Other aspects of the Valente statements Novitzky relates in his memorandum just don't add up. For example, Novitzky says Valente told him that Anderson paid Conte directly for the Clear and the Cream. But this conflicts with the theory that Bonds only "paid" for those substances by promoting the basic zinc and mineral product—ZMA—that was making big money for Conte. Ultimately, Novitzky's notes, unsupported by a tape recording, just don't prove a thing. To a certain extent, they actually raise more questions than they answer.

One of the notable weaknesses in the case against Bonds is the fact that no one has ever come forward to say he or she saw him use steroids. Let's assume for the moment that Conte, Anderson, and Valente had nothing to gain by saying they had observed Bonds using steroids. What if Bonds really was a chronic steroid user, but Conte, Anderson, and Valente just were not close enough to Bonds to actually see him injecting Deca Durabolin or swallowing Stanozolol? Certainly, the perfect witness must exist—a person who has it in for Bonds and, yet, someone who was close enough to Bonds so that it would have been impossible to miss his rampant steroid use. If you have been paying attention, you already know the one person who fits the bill is Bell.

Bell was Bonds's girlfriend from 1994 to 2003. Bell often traveled with Bonds, roomed with Bonds, shared meals with Bonds, and even slept with him. If Bonds was a rampant steroid user, it would have been virtually impossible to avoid injecting or ingesting steroids in front of Bell. Certainly, one would expect Bell to have stumbled across Bonds's steroid stash in a hotel room or in a car at least once, if not 10 or 15 times.

While Bell was in a position to closely observe Bonds, in some ways her testimony becomes even more critical because of her extreme negativity toward Bonds. If she can't convince us that Bonds used steroids, no one can. Bell was a jilted lover who had forfeited a career to make Bonds happy. But like so many others who got close to Bonds, Barry made sure he crushed Bell. (Remember his former agent, Rod Wright?) He humiliated her by taking another mistress and left her in dire financial straits by reneging on a promise to buy her a house. Bell was angry and motivated to do everything she could to get back at Bonds.

If anyone could give us a picture or videotape of Bonds injecting himself with steroids, it was Bell. In 2003 Bell decided she would go after Bonds. However, although Bell may have interesting things to say about alleged tax evasion, she has very little to offer when it comes to the question of whether or not Bonds used steroids.

In this land of urban myths and misinformation by design, there are people who somehow came to believe that Bell said she injected Bonds with steroids. That is a 100 percent falsehood. No one has ever claimed to have shot Bonds full of steroids. Here's what Bell really has to say about Bonds and steroids. First, in 2003, Bell's attorney suggested that unless Bonds paid Bell handsomely, Bonds's use of "supplements"—not steroids—would be revealed to the world. Think about it—here we are in 2003 and the world wants to know if Sosa's 66 home runs, McGwire's 70 home runs, and Bonds's 73 home runs were the product of steroid use. Bell desperately wants money from Bonds, and she has hired an attorney to help her get it. She is irate because Bonds essentially traded her in for a new groupie, leaving her without a suitable job and with an unmanageable set of financial burdens. And Bell's attorney can't use the word steroids in his letter to Bonds? Why not?

The reason Bell and her attorney couldn't outright accuse Bonds of steroid use is simple. They had no evidence that Bonds used steroids. Zero. Not a thing. So the attorney's demand letter used what Bell knew—that Bonds used supplements. But supplements are not steroids, and they are perfectly legal.

When the attorney's demand letter failed to produce the desired results, Bell turned to the more traditional methods of goal achievement. She would use the media to get what she wanted. She would use the media to embarrass Bonds. She combined efforts with Aphrodite Jones to put the squeeze on Bonds. Jones and Bell appeared on *At Large with Geraldo Rivera* in February 2005. Bell was unable to offer hard evidence of steroid use. Nevertheless, she told the TV viewing audience she was "familiar with…all of the changes that occurred in his body…as a result of the intimate relationship that we did have." According to Bell, physical changes that proved Bonds's steroid use "included everything from acne on his back to a great deal of bloating."

This is a woman who spent nine years with Bonds—nine years sharing hotel rooms—nine years traveling with Bonds. Could she say she saw him use steroids just once? No! Not even once! Nine years—and she never once observed Bonds using steroids. Instead, she observed powerful and convincing "evidence" such as back acne and unspecified bloating.

But it gets better. In response to Geraldo's typically insightful questioning, Bell told America she also observed so-called 'roid rage in Bonds. Perhaps unwittingly, Bell was almost hilarious in describing Bonds's purported 'roid rage. This really happened: on national TV, Bell said that when Bonds got mad he would draw his hand back and make it look as if he was going to hit her. He did it "just to see me flinch so that he could laugh about it." *Pathetic* might be the right word for Bell's accusation. Having a laugh when someone flinches might inch toward sadism, but it is miles away from 'roid rage.

In *The Steroid Bible*, Steve Gallaway describes an extreme 'roid rage case:

> Horace K. Williams, a 23-year-old anabolic steroid user, was tried in May 1988 for the brutal murder of the hitchhiker. Williams did not have a violent history, and he did not have any major psychological problems. Williams started using anabolic steroids in order to improve his athletic performance. He played football in high school, and after high school he got into bodybuilding. During his trial Williams described how anabolic steroids changed his behavior. In his initial stage of anabolic steroid use…Williams experienced an increase in confidence, increased ability to ask women out, and a willingness to train harder. As his steroid use increased…Williams became easily agitated into violent behavior, threatened people, felt special powers, and tried to get off steroids but "was so depressed that I thought

I might kill myself if I didn't get back on steroids. I felt like a wimp when I wasn't on steroids." Upon consumption of higher doses…Williams became obsessed with building his body, got into several fights, felt like everyone was afraid of him, turned over 15 cars, wanted to fight everybody, lost most of his friends, and couldn't control his madness. It was in this state of mind that the anabolic steroid–created personality of Horace Williams picked up a hitchhiker, drove him to an empty field, undressed him, beat him to death with a board and a lead pipe, scalped him, shaved the hair off his arms and legs, hung him with a rope, and ran him over repeatedly with his vehicle.

Yes, it's true, that is an *extreme* 'roid rage case. But it isn't all that unique. Take Gordon Kimbrough, a bodybuilder who was convicted of murdering his girlfriend. Relatives said Kimbrough was "meek and shy when not on steroids and short-tempered and violent when he was using them." And more recently, when wrestler Chris "Canadian Crippler" Benoit was implicated in the murder-suicide that took his wife and son's lives, steroids were found in the house. Many blamed 'roid rage.

'Roid rage rarely leads to murder. More typically, a guy experiencing 'roid rage may go from bar to bar looking for a fight, initiating physical confrontation, and accepting all challenges. Another example might be a guy who follows someone who merged a little too closely for eight miles on the freeway, trails the offending vehicle off the freeway, and then beats the driver in a parking lot. But getting a laugh out of making your girlfriend flinch has nothing to do with 'roid rage. Bell's story shows (1) just how far she was willing to go to try to implicate Bonds, and (2) just how little she had to work with.

Bell has little credibility when it comes to her attacks on Bonds. Her 'roid rage accusations are preposterous, and her descriptions of

Bonds's purported physical changes are both vague and trivial. Bell also says Bonds self-diagnosed an arm injury that could be indicative of steroid use. Bonds supposedly told Bell he tore a tricep tendon because steroids made him build muscle too quickly. From the standpoint of a Bonds accuser, this would have been a convenient thing for Bonds to say. Some people believe there is a connection between steroid use and torn triceps. And if you wanted to convict Bonds in the court of public opinion, this is a safe accusation to make. But the accusation raises many questions. Why, for example, is this the one and only time Bonds supposedly told Bell he was using steroids? Or, is it equally likely that Bonds told Bell he thought the injury may have resulted from training too intensely?

Either way, the alleged verbal exchange sounds like something that Bell made up after the fact. It leaves us to wonder why Bonds would make this "confession" and then never mention steroids to Bell again. He never mentioned steroids on his rambling phone messages. He never once asked Bell to inject him with steroids, handle his steroids, or watch him take steroids. She never once saw him with steroids.

And why would Bonds try to diagnose his own injury? Tricep injuries are often caused by falling in a way where the arm ends up supporting most of the body's weight. If Bonds was using steroids but didn't want people to know about it, why not say he hurt his arm diving for a baseball? Or, given the intensity of Bonds's workouts, why not tell people he hurt his arm lifting weights? It seems strange that Bonds would choose this one episode as the basis for disclosing his alleged steroid use to Bell.

Ultimately, Bell's statements suggest that Bonds was not a regular steroid user. Bell was in a prime position to observe Bonds using steroids. Bell was in a prime position to observe (if not confiscate) any steroids Bonds may have been using. The fact that Bell never saw Bonds use steroids (and that she never found any steroids) seems to tell us Bonds was not using steroids.

*

Fainaru-Wada and Williams say Bonds *admitted* that he used steroids when he testified before a grand jury in December 2003. And their take on the grand jury testimony that was so conveniently leaked to them has been repeated by thousands of others, including some who should know better. For example, Curt Schilling recently proclaimed that Bonds "admitted that he used steroids" and "admitted to cheating on his wife, cheating on his taxes, and cheating on the game." Perhaps because there was a noticeable gap between reality and Schilling's comments, the pitcher promptly issued a public apology. As usual, the apology didn't receive the same attention the accusations received.

Grand jury proceedings are supposed to be confidential. Improper disclosure of grand jury testimony is a contempt of court. The *Shadows* authors were never supposed to receive transcripts of Bonds's grand jury testimony, but they say someone allowed them to review the transcripts. For a time, this was a big mystery. The two reporters were prepared to go to jail to maintain the secrecy of the leaker's identity. And that left us guessing—was it Conte? Valente's attorney, Ellerman? A prosecutor? Novitzky? Although it is still possible that more than one leaker existed, Ellerman has stepped forward to take responsibility for the misdeed. Now the mystery involves trying to understand why an attorney and two reporters would work together to publish selected excerpts of grand jury testimony the law required to be kept confidential.

The actual transcripts of Bonds's grand jury testimony have not been made public. Instead, the world has heard the Fainaru-Wada/Williams interpretation of the transcripts. The parts of the transcripts they discuss do not have Bonds answering questions with something along the lines of, "I took steroids, but I thought they were vitamins." According to *Shadows*, Bonds responded to the prosecutors the way he often responded to reporters, by answering a question that wasn't really asked or by trying to redirect the question. Unfortunately, avoiding, recharacterizing, or arguing about questions produces testimony that appears evasive and unreliable.

What exactly did Bonds tell the grand jury? According to *Shadows*, Bonds said he had known Anderson for a long time, and Anderson introduced Bonds to BALCO.

Bonds did not say he used steroids. He spoke about "cream" and flaxseed oil. Could the flaxseed oil really have been flaxseed oil? Some say no one would take flaxseed oil from a needleless syringe. But anyone who has tried to take flaxseed oil knows it can be a messy process. A needleless syringe hardly sounds like the world's stupidest way to take it. So it comes back to Anderson. Although he has faced almost constant pressure to say that he gave Bonds steroids, Anderson has never said that he did. Two undercover operations and one secret tape recording failed to catch Anderson saying that he gave steroids to Bonds. And unfortunately, even if Anderson ultimately elects to testify that he did give Bonds steroids, the testimony would be called into doubt. It would certainly seem possible, if not likely, that Anderson was just telling the government what it wanted to hear so that he would finally be left alone.

But even without Anderson's confirmation, many people see Bonds's grand jury testimony as an admission that he used the Cream and the Clear. That conclusion is really just an assumption. Yet, there is a deeper, more meaningful reason as to why Bonds's grand jury testimony falls short of proving that Bonds tried steroids even one time. Bonds knew the government was interested in pursuing perjury charges. When Bonds and his attorneys arrived at the courthouse the morning he was going to testify, they quickly learned that prosecutors had backed out of a deal that would have allowed Bonds's attorney to review documents pertaining to Bonds that had been compiled by the government during its investigation. Bonds and his attorney, Michael Rains, were naturally outraged. They had very little time to make strategic decisions in terms of how Bonds would approach the testimony.

Lying about a point that is material to a grand jury's investigation can result in a perjury conviction and up to five years' imprisonment. Under federal law, the testimony of a single witness that contradicts the defendant's statements may be enough to support a perjury conviction. This means that even if Bonds never once tried steroids, it was in his interest to say something truthful that would at least partially coincide with whatever testimony others might offer. If Bonds had simply denied using the Cream and the Clear without offering a concession, prosecutors could pursue perjury charges based on circumstantial evidence or testimony from other witnesses who would be expected to say Bonds used substances that looked like the Cream and the Clear—either in order to promote their agenda or to exact a measure of revenge on Bonds.

By acknowledging that he used a cream and took the oil his trainer supplied, Bonds accomplished several important things. First, he established a measure of credibility. A flat-out, full denial might have been much harder to swallow than a few drops of flaxseed oil. So why not say what was undoubtedly true, that his trainer had given him some kind of cream and some kind of oil?

Second, and more important, by telling the grand jury that he used a cream Anderson supplied and oil Anderson provided, Bonds made sure the hurdle the government would have to jump in connection with any perjury case it initiated against him was set fairly high. If Bonds denied applying cream or ingesting oil, or if he had taken the Rafael Palmeiro approach and just flatly denied steroid use, period, federal prosecutors might be tempted to pursue perjury charges if they could prove Anderson gave something to Bonds, even if Bonds had no idea what Anderson was giving him. Bonds's vague testimony meant that the government would have to prove Bonds knew he was getting steroids—the Cream and the Clear. If not, perjury was out of the question. Although the government would have to prove its case beyond a reasonable doubt, Bonds's fear of possible perjury charges seems entirely reasonable. Under the circumstances, it is easy to see that Bonds would have wanted to protect himself against perjury charges by affirmatively mentioning his use of what he assumed to be flaxseed oil and a form of pain relief cream, even if he had never used a steroid.

*

While some have suggested that there is no way Bonds would take something his trainer gave him without knowing exactly what he was using, that point of view is hard to reconcile with what we already know. Actually, when Bonds was playing for Arizona State, Jim Brock, Arizona State's coach, recommended his team take Nardil, an antidepressant. Bonds apparently followed Brock's advice blindly. But the incident made Bonds's father irate. Bobby told Brock he would break his neck if Brock ever gave his son "anything medical again."

More recent history reflects the likelihood that Bonds would take what his trainers gave him without asking questions. Jim Warren worked with Bonds as a trainer in the mid-1990s. Warren reveals that "when I worked with him, Barry took everything I told him to without asking a question." In fact, says Warren, "He wasn't that curious about it all." Warren believes it is quite possible that Bonds took whatever Anderson gave him without asking questions about exactly what kind of cream or oil he was using.

No matter how much a person wants to believe Bonds hit home runs because he used steroids, there are other glaring inadequacies in the existing "proof." For example, Conte told Novitzky that he bought the Clear from Patrick Arnold for a grand total of $450. Conte says $450 worth of the Clear never ran out. It was enough to supply all of his athletes. It is hard to believe that $450 worth of a designer steroid would have gone such a long way if Conte was supplying 27 different athletes. Maybe $450 worth of flaxseed oil would have lasted a while. But $450 worth of the world's most advanced undetectable steroid? If Conte only had $450 worth of the Clear, we can surmise one thing—even if some made its way to Bonds, he could not have taken very many doses.

Arnold won't say exactly how much money he received from Conte, but he has confirmed that Conte bought very little tetrahydrogestrinone (THG). And let's face it, because the underground steroid business is not heavily regulated, the temptation to make money for nothing is great. Fake products masquerading as potent anabolics—but products that actually have little or no steroid content—abound. Why sell someone expensive drugs if they'll pay you just as much for a fake product? Let's not forget, some studies suggest that placebos (or even flaxseed oil?) might work just as well as real steroids. This does not mean Conte necessarily bought fake steroids from Arnold or that he gave placebos to athletes. It just means we really don't know.

Valente, who generally comes across as somewhat credible, told Novitzky that Bonds did not like the way the Clear made him feel. This would be perfectly consistent with the notion that Bonds may have tried the Clear once or twice but decided that it did not work or actually made him feel bad. To the extent Valente was telling the truth, it would be natural for Valente to note that Bonds did not particularly like the Clear. After all, Valente says he tried the Clear himself but didn't like it. Either way, if it cost $450 for an endless supply, the Clear was no miracle drug. And even if Bonds tried it a few times, it doesn't mean he hit even so much as a single home run because he used a designer steroid.

What about the Cream? There is no convincing evidence that Bonds regularly used the Cream. But even if that kind of evidence existed, it would not mean that Bonds hit home runs because he used steroids. The Cream, it turns out, is used as a masking agent more than a muscle builder. *Shadows* explains it this way:

> The Cream was designed to mask use of other steroids. It was a mixture of synthetic testosterone and epitestosterone. Epi, as it was known in the drug-testing culture, was present in the body but had no known function. But it was important to drug testers, who used it to differentiate between natural testosterone and synthetic testosterone in an athlete's body. Normally, epi and testosterone occurred in about a 1:1 ratio. So, a threshold was set—a loose one at that—in which an athlete whose ratio exceeded 6:1 would be considered to be doping. Conte's Cream helped the athlete maintain a normal ratio, and it concealed what otherwise would be a telltale sign of the use of an undetectable steroid: an abnormally low testosterone level. When a person takes steroids, the body stops producing testosterone to the point that it can bottom out at zero. A zero level would set off red flags for drug testers, but the Cream elevated testosterone enough to avoid suspicion.

Steroid testing, of course, is not exactly foolproof. The testing cannot identify actual steroids in the body, but it can identify substances and substance concentrations that are deemed suggestive of possible or likely steroid use. Different types of tests use different methodologies. Simple testosterone ratio tests compare levels of testosterone to epitestosterone. A more complex test tries to analyze carbon isotope ratios in order to determine whether the testosterone came from an external source (i.e., steroids). Tests for specific steroids try to identify quantities of metabolites the steroids are thought to leave behind as they work their way through the body.

Take Floyd Landis. He won the 2006 Tour de France. Temporarily. A testosterone ratio test—the type of test the Cream was designed to foil—suggested Landis did something he wasn't supposed to do before his incredibly impressive performance on the 17th stage. The T / E ratio test that put Landis under suspicion did not generate consistent results. Tests from Landis's "A" sample resulted in testosterone to epitestosterone ratios of 4.9:1 (at the low end) and 11.4:1 (at the high end). That's a very big divergence. (A third test yielded a 5.1:1 ratio.) If we assume that valid "positive" test results are a strong indicator of steroid use, it is still important to remember that testing is only as good as the laboratory equipment, practices, and technicians who do the testing. On September 20, 2007, an arbitration panel voted two to one against Landis, stripping him of his Tour de France title. All three arbitrators believed the lab's practices were so deficient that the simple testosterone ratio testing was not reliable. Nevertheless, two of the arbitrators felt carbon ratio isotope testing that same lab performed was good enough for government work, so to speak, and good enough to justify ruling against Landis.

By boosting an athlete's epitestosterone levels, the Cream might help to thwart the simple ratio testing that was ultimately deemed unreliable in Landis's case. But if the Cream was primarily used as a masking agent it probably wasn't going to help Barry Bonds (or any other athlete) build much muscle or hit home runs.

8

Closing Thoughts

Remember the commercial Charles Schwab ran a few years ago? Barry Bonds is alone in an empty baseball stadium at night, practicing his hitting. A voice whispers in the distance, "Barry Bonds, it's time. It's time to walk into retirement." The voice goes on to ask, "Why hang around just to break the all-time home-run record?" Bonds stops and looks back toward the press box. Then he says, "Hank, would you cut it out already?" Then we see Hank Aaron asking, "Hank who?" Aaron not only agreed to film the commercial, but he has openly encouraged Bonds to try to break his career home-run record. According to Aaron, "Records are meant to be broken." Aaron boldly said, "I have complete and utmost confidence that Barry is as clean as a whistle. I don't have any doubt in my mind." Aaron went on to say that what Bonds has "done these past few years has strictly been because he's very talented and is capable of doing it. I don't think there's anybody who can take that away from him." But Aaron has also acknowledged that he is in a no-win situation. Right now, the public's mind closely associates Bonds with steroids. So it is almost as if Aaron can't support Bonds without being accused of supporting illegal performance-enhancing drugs.

In *When Winning Costs Too Much*, John McCloskey and Julian Bailes suggest that a 2004 newspaper article shows that Aaron shares their belief that Bonds should be removed from the record books because of his alleged steroid use. Their assessment of the article is not quite fair. The article itself invites questions as to its accuracy. In a February 29, 2004, *New York Daily News* article, Bill Madden relays a few purported Aaron quotes. He also says Aaron "never hit more than 45 homers in a season." Well, not exactly. Don't we have to count 1971 as a season? And didn't Aaron hit 47 home runs that year?

But the major problem is not Madden's minor errors, it is the distortion of Aaron's statements. Aaron *did* say that the inquiry into steroids threatened the game. He did *not* say he believed Bonds used steroids. And he did *not* say Bonds should be stripped of his records. What Aaron told Madden was that "I won't mind if somebody breaks [my record]." What Aaron told Madden was that "when I played we didn't have the weight-training programs they do today. I was told that lifting weights would be detrimental to my swing. I never lifted a weight in my life."

That's a far cry from saying "Barry Bonds used steroids, and if he breaks my record I'm still the only legitimate home-run king." But if you've already made up your mind, you can probably make Aaron's words mean anything you want them to mean.

The tendency to stretch the truth to get at Bonds is one reason so many people who casually follow baseball believe Bonds obviously cheated. The distortion happens with enough frequency to help explain why so many are so eager to assume Bonds used steroids, and that steroids are responsible for all of those home runs. When people who get paid to think about this stuff can't separate fact from fiction, how can we expect more from a general public that only has time to read the headlines?

But we can do better if we focus on what we actually know. The known evidence against Bonds is questionable. The single piece of "evidence" that convinced so many is both inaccurate and false. Bonds never gained 40 pounds of muscle in a single off-season. In fact, he never gained 30 or even 20 pounds in a single off-season. Bonds has never tested positive for steroids. No person has ever said he or she injected Bonds with steroids. Bonds does not act like a person on steroids. While he has always been mean-spirited, he has never demonstrated the symptoms of 'roid rage. His former mistress, a woman who really wants to nail him, can't say she ever saw Bonds with steroids—not even once.

In January 2007, T.J. Quinn of the *New York Daily News* reported that Bonds had failed one test in 2006—a test for amphetamines, not steroids. Amphetamines are a form of the "greenies" Jim Bouton mentions in *Ball Four*. They have been around forever, and they help players to stay alert, not to build muscle or hit home runs. Amphetamines are stimulants, akin to caffeine. Baseball's punishment for a first failed test is treatment and counseling. If it actually happened, the positive amphetamine test subjects Bonds to additional testing.

Pete Rose admitted his use of greenies in a 1979 interview with *Playboy* magazine. Some say greenies are what made Charlie Hustle. Ken Caminiti said greenies were really beneficial for players who had been drinking heavily the night before a game. Greenies and other stimulants have been so popular for so long that players describe playing without taking stimulants as "playing naked."

If we condemn Bonds for taking stimulants, we might as well close down baseball. We would probably be condemning at least 50 percent of the people who played professional baseball between 1965 and 2005. Even if Bonds took stimulants, amphetamines, or greenies, it doesn't mean he deserves an asterisk. It doesn't mean that he loses his rightful place in the Hall of Fame.

Tests for stimulants really don't deserve our attention. But steroid tests do. Or at least they should. What if Bonds's steroid-test results are subsequently revealed as negative? Will people finally back off and stop calling him a chronic steroid-using cheater? Of course not. At most, negative test results would merely be one more small piece of evidence (among many pieces of such evidence) suggesting that Bonds hit home runs because he was talented, not because of steroids.

Bonds has worked incredibly hard—harder than any other major league baseball player. He has been more single-minded in his pursuit of greatness than any other player ever was. Bonds does not relate well to people. But his baseball IQ is off the charts. He has gained weight. He has lifted weights and built muscle. He has refined his swing and batting eye so that he is able to hit more home runs and draw more walks. His body is consistent with gradual weight gain and a singular dedication to weight training.

When the available information is more closely scrutinized, it is easy to see that the case against Bonds is relatively weak, not particularly convincing, and built on a series of unfounded assumptions, exaggerations, and recklessly speculative conclusions.

On the other hand, Bonds's reputation for mistreating others is almost as legendary as his ability to hit a baseball. And Bonds is paying the price. Because so many would enjoy seeing Bonds fall and fall hard, it takes little to convince them that Bonds cheated by regularly using steroids and that his statistical success is a direct result of incessant steroid use. So it may already be too late for Bonds to win an appeal in the court of public opinion, regardless of the truth. Once minds are made up they can easily make new factual information fit right along with old assumptions. Bonds may have believed he could treat people any way he wanted as long as he performed. If Bonds's only goal was to amass astonishingly superior statistics, his belief was accurate. But if Bonds wanted more—if he wanted the public to appreciate his success—it would have been wise for Bonds to treat other people with some degree of respect, if not a little admiration, once in a while.

*

Five years after he stops playing baseball Bonds will be eligible for the Hall of Fame. Voting is "based upon the player's record, playing ability, integrity, sportsmanship, character, and contributions to the team(s) on which the player played." If Bonds did not use steroids his election to the Hall of Fame is a slam dunk. As a fielder Bonds was good enough to win eight Gold Gloves. As a speedster, Bonds has stolen more than 500 bases, more than Aaron, Babe Ruth, and Duke Snider combined. By 2004 Bonds had arguably surpassed Ruth, becoming the most potent offensive force in the history of the game. Bonds was *intentionally* walked 120 times in 2004. Opposing teams were so reluctant to pitch to Bonds that he drew 232 walks that season. In 2002 he drew 198 walks. Ruth never walked more than 170 times in a single season. Bonds hit a record 73 home runs in 2001. Did you ever doubt that he would surpass Aaron as the career home-run leader? Statistically speaking Bonds would be grouped with Babe Ruth, Ted Williams, Ty Cobb, and Rogers Hornsby. If an all-time team was assembled, Bonds would be the starting left fielder.

But voting is also based on integrity, sportsmanship, and character. Bonds did not treat fans, the press, or his teammates particularly well. Over the years, he has said and done some stupid things. But Bonds isn't the only spoiled athlete who treated people inappropriately. According to Bouton, Mickey Mantle refused to sign baseballs and got angry at people way too easily and way too frequently. Bouton recalled "all those times" Mantle would "push little kids aside when they wanted his autograph," and how he was "snotty to reporters, just about making them crawl and beg for a minute of his time." Sound familiar?

Hornsby may have been the greatest right-handed hitter in the history of baseball, with 301 home runs and a lifetime batting average of .358. His personality, however, was quirky. According to teammate George "Specs" Toporczer, Hornsby "kept distinctly aloof from his teammates," was "hard to approach," and seemed "to have nothing but contempt for the usual likes and dislikes of the average player."

Some people think Hornsby was at least briefly a Ku Klux Klan member.

Other Hall of Famers raised bad conduct to levels Mantle, Hornsby, and Bonds could never imagine. Comparing Cobb to Bonds would be like comparing a mafia hit man to a guy who has a paying job but applies for unemployment benefits anyway. We are talking about two entirely different levels of badness.

Cobb was an original Hall of Fame inductee. He played 24 seasons and retired with the game's highest lifetime batting average (.366). Cobb stole 892 bases. He had 4,189 base hits. He scored 2,246 runs and drove in another 1,937.

Character did not stop Cobb from taking his rightful place in the Hall of Fame. Even by the standards of his era, Cobb was a maniac with an incredibly ugly personality. Ernest Hemingway summed him up nicely when he said, "Ty Cobb, the greatest of all ballplayers—and an absolute shit." According to some, Cobb was a bitter racist who had actually chased down and killed a person who had initiated a conflict. He once kicked a black woman in the stomach, knocking her down several stairs, because she didn't react too cheerfully after Cobb called her the *N* word.

Although Cobb tried to explain it as a situation where he was just a middle man for another player's bet, documentary evidence suggested that Cobb bet on baseball and may have participated in a plan to fix at least one game during the 1919 season (the same year the White Sox threw the World Series to the Reds and saw eight of their players banned from baseball for life). In fact, Cobb's own letter referred to "our business proposition."

In 1912 Cobb went after a fan who was heckling him during a game. The fan, Claude Lueker, had been involved in an unfortunate accident that left him with no fingers on one hand and only two on the other. The handicap didn't stop Cobb from landing more than 10 punches to Lueker's head. When Lueker finally went down, Cobb started kicking him. Nearby fans were horrified and yelling out that the man Cobb was beating had no hands. Cobb yelled back at them, "I don't care if he has no legs!"

Cobb received more votes than Ruth (or anyone else) when he was elected to the Hall of Fame in 1936 with 98.23 percent of the ballots. Compared to Cobb, Bonds is an angel.

Despite (or perhaps, because of) his unusual personality, baseball has never known a harder working or more dedicated player than Bonds. Absent convincing evidence that Bonds was a chronic steroid user, he should be unanimously elected to the Hall of Fame.

When it is closely scrutinized and carefully evaluated, the so-called proof of Bonds's alleged steroid use is shockingly thin and surprisingly flimsy. To a significant extent the "evidence" of Bonds's steroid use is flawed. In some instances it is significantly inaccurate.

Membership in the Hall of Fame is not a citizenship award—it is, instead, the ultimate recognition of the player's superior ability. Gaylord Perry was a good pitcher. He won 314 games during his 22-year career. The first year he pitched for the Cleveland Indians was 1972. He won 24 games and had a 1.92 earned-run average. Two years later Perry published his autobiography of sorts, titled *Me and the Spitter*. In the book, Perry bragged about how he had consistently broken the rules by throwing baseballs that were adulterated with human saliva, or worse. He claimed he was so practiced, he could break the rules without detection despite the closest scrutiny. His spitball had an extremely sharp downward break that consistently fooled hitters.

Without the spitter—an illegal pitch that directly violated baseball's official rules—Perry was a mediocre major league pitcher, at best. With the spitter, Perry was great, and he was inducted into the Hall of Fame in 1991. Perry's book did equivocate a little. Although he explained the excruciating details of throwing the spitball, Perry also said, "Do I still wet them? I sure know how.

But that doesn't mean I do it—or even that I ever did it. Maybe I'm just kidding."

Perry won the Cy Young Award in 1972 and in 1978, four years after he published his book. There is no asterisk by his name in the record books. And there should never be an asterisk next to Barry Bonds's name, either.

Did Perry's contemporaries hate him? A few did. But Dick Allen said, "He can play on my team anytime." And Luis Aparicio said it would "be an honor" to "watch him work." Since Perry is in the Hall of Fame, it is kind of crazy to even think about keeping Bonds out.

Even if he was a chronic steroid user after 1998, even if steroids doubled Bonds's productivity from 1998 to 2003 (when baseball implemented steroid testing), Bonds belongs in the Hall of Fame. He would still have more than 600 home runs and more than 450 stolen bases. He would still have eight Gold Gloves. He would still possess a remarkably high baseball IQ. And he would still be the hardest working and most dedicated player of the era.

But we are a long way away from debating the issue. The existing evidence of Bonds's alleged chronic steroid use is unconvincing. More than anything else, the "evidence" and the public's reaction to it proves that Bonds is not well liked. It proves that people who don't like the way Bonds treated people are willing to work hard to try to convince others that Bonds was a chronic steroid user. And it tells us that a lot of people are very anxious to believe bad things about Barry Bonds.

Let's get a little perspective—Bonds was often extremely rude when he spoke to people. He came across as stingy, selfish, and mean-spirited. But Bonds wasn't betting on baseball. Bonds doesn't go into the stands to fight with fans. He doesn't hang out at strip clubs drinking until 3:00 in the morning and then try to outrun the cops on his way home. He just works hard, shows up, and occasionally says some mean and stupid things. But he also hits a baseball better than anyone else ever has.

Is it okay to hate Barry Bonds? If the accounts of the way he has mistreated people are anywhere close to true, you certainly have my permission. But don't let that hate get the best of you. Don't hate his game. Don't hate his talent. Don't hate his work ethic.

If your feelings push you to conclude that Bonds was a chronic steroid user before you carefully evaluate the available information on both sides of the issue, you're only cheating yourself.

Postscript

On November 15, 2007, the federal government indicted Barry Bonds. Greg Anderson, whose testimony apparently wasn't so critical after all, was released from prison. The indictment had four perjury counts and one obstruction of justice count. The tax evasion charges so many expected never materialized. Still, theoretically, Bonds could spend up to 30 years in prison if he gets convicted.

The public reaction was immediate and expected: Bonds got so big so fast it was always obvious that he was a chronic steroid user and a human growth hormone abuser. So he had to be lying if he didn't tell prosecutors that Greg Anderson was shooting him full of steroids. Conviction was inevitable. The greatest hitter of our time would never play baseball again. The Hall of Fame was out of the question. Bonds was finally getting what he deserved. Yes, maybe a lot of players tried steroids, but Bonds set the records. So if he ends up being the only major league baseball player who does jail time because of steroids, that's OK. In other words, much of the public and its media representatives continued to assume Bonds was guilty as charged.

There were, of course, a lot of facts no one was talking about. No one mentioned that Bonds weighed as much as 220 pounds *before* the 1998 season started. No one mentioned that the long term "mistress" who was out to get Bonds had never seen him use or even possess steroids. No one mentioned that the undercover sting operations that had been aimed at Greg Anderson had come up empty. No one mentioned that Bonds had improved his bench press from 230 to 315 pounds by the middle of the 1996. No one was talking about the fact that Bonds's accusers couldn't agree on when he allegedly started using steroids, or when he "suddenly got huge." And no one was trying to figure out why Mark Silva hadn't had to change the mold of Bonds's right arm (for his custom built elbow pad) since 1995.

The indictment mentions "positive tests for the presence of anabolic steroids and other performance-enhancing substances." The details behind the tests were not disclosed. However, parts of the indictment suggest that the positive tests were probably informal, with samples provided through BALCO. So it may be difficult for the government to establish that the testing was performed on properly handled samples that actually originated from Barry Bonds. Bonds says he first saw the test paperwork when he testified.

How strong is the government's case? Federal prosecutors know what they're doing and they don't like to lose cases. Yet, not every prosecutor who looked at this case felt it was rock solid—at least not without Greg Anderson's testimony. If we assume that the government will ultimately be able to prove that Bonds was a regular steroid user and that he knew Greg Anderson was giving him (or injecting him with) illegal steroids, a possible conviction still faces other significant hurdles. Generally speaking, even a potentially evasive answer cannot support a perjury conviction if it is technically true. The questioning has to be precise and specific.

This is from Count Two of the indictment:

> Q: And did he [Anderson] ever give you anything that he told you had to be taken with a needle or syringe?
>
> A: Greg wouldn't do that. He knows I'm against that stuff. So, he would never come up to me—he would never jeopardize our friendship like that.

Q: So, just so I'm clear, the answer is no to that, he never gave you anything like that?

A: Right.

The exchange is a bit ambiguous. The initial question seems to concentrate on what Anderson told Bonds about the substances he was giving him. But the subsequent question could be mixing two different issues, asking about the answer to the prior question regarding what Anderson told Bonds, but then switching its focus in mid-sentence to what Anderson gave Bonds, not what he said about it. The reference to "anything like that" may not be enough to precisely clarify the question Bonds was called on to answer. Undoubtedly, Bonds's attorneys will closely scrutinize all of the questioning that led to the indictment.

The indictment means that the court of public opinion is no longer paramount. The government will have to prove the case with solid evidence. It won't be able to rely on the string of shaky evidence that has managed to convince so many people that Bonds is a monster who obviously abused steroids. If Bonds is acquitted, it won't prove that he never used steroids. It will just mean the government didn't have the evidence to prove its case. If Bonds is convicted, it will not prove that he hit home runs because he used steroids, and it may not keep him out of the Hall of Fame. But either way, the indictment assures that Bonds will remain the leading symbol of baseball's steroid era. Win or lose, Bonds will suffer far more than anyone else for the perceived sins of that era.

The steroid controversy got even more interesting a week after Bonds proclaimed his innocence in court. On December 13, 2007, the long-anticipated Mitchell Report appeared. Bonds suddenly had some company. The report linked more than 80 players and former players to steroids, HGH, or other "performance enhancers."

Mitchell urged the Commissioner to refrain from punishing those players who were mentioned in the report, "except in those cases where he determines that the conduct is so serious that discipline is necessary to maintain the integrity of the game." Barry Bonds must still feel very lonely.

References

Books

Adair, Robert K. *The Physics of Baseball.* New York, New York: Perennial, 2002.

Alexander, Charles C. *Rogers Hornsby: A Biography.* New York, New York: Henry Holt & Company, 1995.

Asinof, Eliot. *Eight Men Out.* New York, New York: Henry Holt & Company, 1963.

Barra, Allen. *Clearing the Bases: The Greatest Baseball Debates of the Last Century.* New York, New York: Thomas Dunne Books, 2002.

Becker, Jill B., Breedlove, Marc, and Crews, David, *Behavioral Endocrinology,* Cambridge, Mass: The MIT Press, 1992.

Bissinger, Buzz. *Three Nights in August.* Boston, Massachusetts: Mariner Books, 2005.

Bloom, John. *Barry Bonds: A Biography.* Westport, Connecticut: Greenwood Press, 2004.

Bouton, Jim. *Ball Four.* New York, New York: Dell Publishing,1970.

———. *Ball Four: The Final Pitch.* Champaign, Illinois: Sports Publishing, 2000.

Bradbury, J.C., *The Baseball Economist,* New York: Dutton, 2007.

Bryant, Howard. *Juicing the Game.* New York, New York: Plume, 2005.

Canseco, José. *Juiced.* New York, New York: Regan Books, 2005.

Carroll, Will. *The Juice: The Real Story of Baseball's Drug Problems.* Chicago, Illinois: Ivan R. Dee, 2005.

Collins, Rick. *Legal Muscle: Anabolics in America*. East Meadow, New York: Legal Muscle Publishing, 2002.

Creamer, Robert W. *Babe: The Legend Comes to Life*. New York: Fireside, 1974.

Dorfman, H.A., and Karl Kuehl. *The Mental Game of Baseball*. Lanham, Maryland: Diamond Communications, 1995.

Draper, Robert, *Dead Certain: The Presidency of George W. Bush*, New York: Free Press, 2007.

Fainaru-Wada, Mark, and Lance Williams. *Game of Shadows*. New York, New York: Gotham Books, 2006.

Gallaway, Steve. *The Steroid Bible*. Honolulu, Hawaii: Belle International, 1997.

Gay, Timothy M. *Tris Speaker: The Rough-and-Tumble Life of a Baseball Legend*. Omaha, Nebraska: University of Nebraska Press, 2005.

Gilbert, Brother. *Young Babe Ruth*. Edited by Harry Rothgerber. Jefferson, North Carolina: McFarland, 1999.

Golenbock, Peter. *The Spirit of St. Louis: A History of the St. Louis Cardinals and Browns*. New York, New York: HarperCollins, 2000.

James, Bill. *The Bill James Historical Baseball Abstract*. New York, New York: Villard Books, 1988.

James, Bill, *Whatever Happened to the Hall of Fame*, New York: Simon & Schuster (1995).

Jendrick, Nathan. *Dunks, Doubles, Doping: How Steroids Are Killing American Athletics*. Guilford, Connecticut: The Lyons Press, 2006.

Jenkinson, Bill. *The Year Babe Ruth Hit 104 Home Runs*. New York, New York: Carroll & Graf, 2007.

Kaat, Jim. *Still Pitching*. Chicago, Illinois: Triumph Books, 2003.

Keating, Peter. *Dingers*. New York, New York: ESPN Publishing, 2006.

Kelly, Kitty. *The Family: The Real Story of the Bush Dynasty*. New York, New York: Doubleday, 2004.

Keri, Jonah. *Baseball Between the Numbers*. New York, New York: Basic Books, 2006.

Kiner, Ralph. *Baseball Forever: Reflections on 60 Years in the Game*. Chicago, Illinois: Triumph Books, 2004.

Kittle, Ron. *Ron Kittle's Tales from the White Sox Dugout*. Champaign, Illinois: Sports Publishing, 2005.

Koppett, Leonard. *Koppett's Concise History of Major League Baseball*. New York, New York: Carroll & Graf Publishers, 2004.

Landis, Floyd, *Positively False*, New York: Simon Spotlight Entertainment (2007).

Leavy, Jane. *Sandy Koufax: A Lefty's Legacy*. New York, New York: Perennial, 2002.

Letarte, Richard H. *That One Glorious Season*. Portsmouth, New Hampshire: Peter E. Randall Publisher, 2006.

Lightsey, David. *Muscles, Speed & Lies: What the Sport Supplement Industry Does Not Want Athletes or Consumers to Know*. Guilford, Connecticut: The Lyons Press, 2006.

Mazzone, Leo. *Leo Mazzone's Tales from the Mound*. Champaign, Illinois: Sports Publishing, 2006.

McCloskey, John, and Julian Bailes. *When Winning Costs Too Much*. Lanham, Maryland: Taylor Trade Publishing, 2005.

McConnell, Bob, and David Vincent. *The Home Run Encyclopedia*. New York, New York: MacMillan, 1996.

Montville, Leigh. *The Big Bam*. New York, New York: Doubleday, 2006.

———. *Ted Williams: The Biography of an American Hero*. New York, New York: Doubleday, 2004.

Morgan, Joe. *Long Balls, No Strikes*. New York, New York: Random House, 1999.

Morris, Peter. *A Game of Inches: The Story Behind the Innovations That Shaped Baseball*. Chicago, Illinois: Ivan R. Dee, 2006.

Pearlman, Jeff. *Love Me, Hate Me: Barry Bonds and the Making of an Antihero.* New York, New York: HarperCollins, 2006.

Perry, Gaylord. *Me and the Spitter.* Toronto, Canada: Clarke, Irwin & Co., 1974.

Pettit, Bob. *Bob Pettit: The Drive Within Me.* Englewood Cliffs, New Jersey: Prentice Hall, 1966.

Pound, Dick. *Inside Dope.* Mississauga, Ontario: Wiley, 2006.

Reisler, Jim. *Babe Ruth: Launching the Legend.* New York, New York: McGraw-Hill, 2004.

Roberts, Anthony, and Brian Clapp. *Anabolic Steroids Ultimate Research Guide.* Vol. 1. Montgomery, Texas: Anabolic Information, 2005.

Rose, Pete, *My Prison Without Bars*, Emmaus, Pennsylvania: Rodale, 2004.

Rose, Pete, and Roger Kahn. *Pete Rose: My Story.* New York, New York: Macmillan, 1989.

Ross, Ken. *Mathematician at the Ballpark: Odds and Probabilities for Baseball Fans.* Chicago, Illinois: Pearson Education, 2004.

Rutstein, Jeff. *The Steroid Deceit: A Body Worth Dying For.* Boston, Massachusetts: Custom Fitness Publishing, 2005.

Stump, Al. *Cobb: A Biography.* Chapel Hill, North Carolina: Algonquin Books, 1994.

Savage, Jeff. *Barry Bonds.* Minneapolis, Minnesota: Lerner Sports, 2004.

Schmidt, Mike. *Clearing the Bases.* New York, New York: HarperCollins, 2006.

Sheffield, Gary. *Inside Power.* New York, New York: Crown Publishers, 2007.

Sowell, Mike. *The Pitch That Killed.* Chicago, Illinois: Ivan R. Dee, 1989.

Stanton, Tom. *Hank Aaron and the Home Run That Changed America.* New York, New York: HarperCollins, 2004.

Suchon, Josh. *This Gracious Season: Barry Bonds & the Greatest Year in Baseball.* Winter Publications, 2002.

Temple, Bob. *Mark McGwire.* The Child's World, 2001.

Thomas, John, ed. *Drugs, Athletes and Physical Performance.* San Antonio, Texas: Plenum Medical Book Company, 1988.

Travers, Steven. *Barry Bonds: Baseball's Superman.* Champaign, Illinois: Sports Publishing, 2002.

Trucks, Rob. *The Catcher.* Cincinatti, Ohio: Emmis Books, 2005.

Vizquel, Omar, *Omar!: My Life On and Off the Field*, Cleveland: Gray & Company, 2002.

Wadler, Gary I., and Brian Hainline. *Drugs and the Athlete.* Philadelphia, Pennsylvania: F.A. Davis Company, 1989.

Walsh, David, *From Lance to Landis*, New York: Ballentine Books, 2007.

Wells, David. *Perfect I'm Not.* New York, New York: Perennial Currents, 2003.

Willey, Warren, *Better Than Steroids*, Victoria, BC, Canada: Trafford, 2007.

Yesalis, Charles E., ed. *Anabolic Steroids in Sport and Exercise.* Champaign, Illinois: Human Kinetics, 1993.

Yesalis, Charles E., and Virginia S. Cowart. *The Steroids Game.* Champaign, Illinois: Human Kinetics, 1998.

Zumsteg, Derek, *The Cheater's Guide to Baseball*, Boston, Mass.: Houghton Mifflin Company, 2007.

Articles

Abrams, Jonathan, His Hometown is Watching Bonds, *Los Angeles Times*, June 26, 2007.

Ackman, Dan. "He Is the Boston Red Sox's Sultan of Statistical Analysis." *The Wall Street Journal*, June 20, 2007.

Adami, Hugh, Choose Your Weapon, Barry, *The Ottawa Citizen*, July 31, 2007.

Anderson, Mark. "Challenge Loses 1–2 Punch: McGwire Eliminated, Sosa Ill." *Las Vegas Review Journal*, February 13, 2000.

Antonen, Mel. "Bonds Loves Freedom and Family, Not Fame." *USA Today*, August 17, 2001. www.usatoday.com.

Ballard, Chris. "Living with Barry: What San Franciscans Think of Bonds." *Sports Illustrated*, May 21, 2007.

Barra, Allen. "Barry and the Babe." *Salon*, October 25, 2002, www.salon.com.

Barth, Julian. "Should Men Still Go Bald Gracefully?" *The Lancet*, January 15, 2000.

Baxter, Kevin. "20/20 Vision? You Might Just Be Batting Average." *Los Angeles Times*, April 23, 2007.

Bernardino, Mike. "A Historian Makes the Argument That Had He Played Today, Babe Ruth's Home Run Totals Would Be Untouchable." *Sun-Sentinel* (Fort-Lauderdale, Florida), May 10, 2006.

Bialik, Carl. "Floyd Landis's Alcohol Defense." *The Wall Street Journal*, August 2, 2006.

Birchard, Karen. "Why Doctors Should Worry About Doping in Sports." *The Lancet*, July 4, 1998.

"Bonds Stirs Fans' Emotions: Booed or Cheered, Home Run Hitter Could Care Less," *Grand Rapid Press* (Mich.), April 8, 2007.

Bondy, Filip. "As Man, Bonds Gets Asterisk. Can't Catch Ruth, Aaron." *New York Daily News*, May 1, 2006.

Borden, Sam. "Reggie Is Mr. Mum: Yanks Issue Gag Order on Heavy Hitter." *New York Daily News*, March 12, 2004.

Brennan, Christine. "Bonds' Return Not Happy for Many." *USA Today*, September 8, 2005.

Brown, Sonya K. and Shalita, A. R., "Acne Vulgaris," *The Lancet*, June 20, 1998.

Calao, A., and G. Lombardi, "Growth-Hormone and Prolactin Excess." *The Lancet*, October 31, 1998.

"Caminiti Comes Clean." *Sports Illustrated*, May 28, 2002, www.sportsillustrated.cnn.com.

"Cardinals DE Berry (Torn Triceps) Done for Season." *Associated Press*, November 20, 2006.

Carlson, Scott. "Hair Salon Chain Owner to Buy Hair Club for Men, Women." *Pioneer Press* (St. Paul, Minnesota), November 16, 2004.

Carroll, Will. "Bonds: The Failed Experiment." April 7, 2006, www.mindandmuscle.net.

Carroll, Wll, Barry Bonds' Brace, *Baseball Prospectus*, Aug. 7, 2007.

Carroll, Will, and Thomas Gorman. "Inside Tommy John Surgery: Thirty Years of Fixing Pitchers." *Baseball Prospectus*, September 22, 2004, www.baseballprospectus.com.

Chapin, Dwight. "The Selling of Barry Bonds—by Barry Bonds." *The San Francisco Chronicle*, June 8, 2004.

Chass, Murray, "Bonds in Peril as His Accuser Goes Public," *The New York Times*, Mar. 31, 2005.

Chass, Murray, "Refusal to Answer raises Questions," *The New York Times*, July 31, 2007.

Christie, James, Say it Ain't So, Lance, *The Globe and Mail* (Canada), Aug. 27, 2005.

Coates, Pete. "Historian Discounts Feats by Bonds: Bill Jenkinson Says the Giants' Slugger Would Have Struggled in the Days of Babe Ruth." *The Ottawa Citizen*, September 29, 2001.

Cole, Matthew, "Who's in Charge Here?," *ESPN The Magazine*, October 8, 2007.

Crasnick, Jerry. "Long Distance Call." *ESPN The Magazine*. www.sports.espn.go.com.

———. "Pitchers' Advantage Is Lost with Batters Wearing Armor." *The Seattle Times*, June 18, 2000.

Curiel, Jonathan, "756's Owner Blames League for Steroids," *San Francisco Chronicle*, Sept. 20, 2007.

Curr, Jack, "Why Bonds Will Never Have to Borrow a Bat," *The New York Times*, July 28, 2007.

Davidoff, Ken. "Man of the Year: Thanks to the Silence of Bonds' Trainer Anderson, We'll All Be Getting Our Punishment." *Newsday*, December 24, 2006.

Dickey, Glenn. "Barry Bonds: A Star Who Doesn't Compromise." *The San Francisco Chronicle*, April 29, 1996.

DiGiovanna, "Bonds Controversy Never Rests," *Los Angeles Times*, July 26, 2007.

Dodd, Mike. "Tommy John Surgery: Pitcher's Best Friend." *USA Today*, July 28, 2003, www.usatoday.com.

Dohrmann, George. "Is This Dr. Evil." *Sports Illustrated*, October 9, 2006.

Egan, Kelly, "Bonds Pays Holman Bat,"*The Ottawa Citizen*, Jan. 27, 2002.

Egelko, Bob. "Bail Denied for Bonds Ex-Trainer." *The San Francisco Chronicle*, July 15, 2006.

Egelko, Bob, "Bonds' Trainer Back Behind Bars," *San Francisco Chronicle*, Aug. 29, 2006.

Egelko, Bob, "Prosecutor Who Pursued Reporters Speaks Out," *San Francisco Chronicle*, Aug. 13, 2007.

Fainaru-Wada, Mark, "Federal Agents Raid Illinois Lab Linked to BALCO Steroid," *San Francisco Chronicle*, Sept. 30, 2005.

Fainaru-Wada, Mark, and Lance Williams. "Agent of Change." *Sports Illustrated*, June 19, 2006.

Gare, Joyce, "Holman Prefers Bonds to Data," *The Ottawa Citizen*, March 22, 2002.

Geller, Andy, "Juice Went Out of Bonds' Sex Life," *The New York Post*, Oct. 4, 2007.

Gerber, James. "Bodybuilders Beware: Perils of Andro Possible." *Healthnotes Newswire*, November 16, 2000, www.emersonecologics.com.

Gross, Daniel. "How to Make the Deficit Look Smaller Than It Is." *The New York Times*, November 23, 2003.

"Headgear for Players," *The New York Times*, Aug. 19, 1920.

Henning, Lynn, "Sheffield Fights Steroid Accusation," *The Detroit News*, July 26, 2007.

Hersh, Philip. "'Ecstatic' Jones Cleared of Doping Charges." *Chicago Tribune*, September 7, 2006.

Hoffer, Richard. "The Importance of Being Barry: The Giants' Barry Bonds Is the Best Player in the Game Today—Just Ask Him." *Sports Illustrated*, May 24, 1993.

Hohlfeld, Neil. "Astros Summary." *The Houston Chronicle*, May 19, 1994.

Hoover, Ken. "Sun Bonds Tells Court Barry Beat Her Often." *The San Francisco Chronicle*, December 7, 1995.

Hunt, Amber. "Sales Rock for Instrument of Tiger's Injury." *Detroit Free Press*, December 15, 2006.

Jenkins, Lee, "One fan Follows a Slugger's Chase from Behind Bars," *The New York Times*, Aug. 8, 2007.

Jenkins, Chris. "Neither Quentin nor Bonds Should Expect to Take over Inner Half." *Sign on San Diego*, May 4, 2003, www.signonsandiego.com.

Jenkins, Paul. "Doping in Sport." *The Lancet,* July 13, 2002.

Johnson, Greg, "Bonds Market is Nonexistent," *Los Angeles Times*, July 11, 2007.

Keown, Tim. "Giants Find Offense, Rip Cardinals." *The San Francisco Chronicle*, June 6, 1994.

Kessler, Robert, "Drug Plea Sends Shock Wave," *Newsday*, April 28, 2007.

Knapp, Gwen. "A Big Confession: I Lied About Bonds." *The San Francisco Chronicle*, February 24, 2005.

———. "A Fan in Denial, or Just a Little Bit Vile?," *The San Francisco Chronicle*, July 17, 2007.

———."What, Me Worry?—Barry Unlikely to Sue Because He's Have to Talk," *San Francisco Chronicle*, Aug. 16, 2007.

———. "Sentence: Business as Usual." *The San Francisco Chronicle,* October 19, 2005.

———. "Inside Club Fed: A Lot of Inmates Want Anderson's Autograph." *The San Francisco Chronicle,* April 22, 2007.

Kubatko, Rock, "Palmer Says Steroids May have Aided 50-HR Anderson in '96," *The Baltimore Sun,* March 16, 2004.

Lapointe, Joe. "As 50 Nears, Franco Feels Forever Young." *The New York Times,* May 23, 2005.

"Leaker in BALCO Case is Sentenced,"*Los Angeles Times,* July 13, 2007.

Lemire, Joe, "The Evolution of Barry Bonds," *Sports Illustrated,* Aug. 13, 2007.

Littman, Jonathan. "Gunning for the Big Guy." *Playboy,* May 2004.

Madden, Bill. "Beantown Blabbermouth." *New York Daily News,* May 13, 2007.

———. "Aaron: I'm Sad for Baseball." *New York Daily News,* February 29, 2004.

Mair, Scott D., et al. "Triceps Tendon Ruptures in Professional Football Players," 32 *The American Journal of Sports Medicine* 431 (2004).

Mariotti, Jay, "Say it Ain't So—Again: Feel-Good Story of Cardinals' Ankiel Looks Like It's Disintegrating Into Yet Another Tale of Performance-Enhancing Drug Use," *Chicago Sun Times,* Sept. 8, 2007.

"McGwire's Testimony Leaves Doubts." *CBS News.* March 18, 2005, www.cbsnews.com.

McNeal, Stan. "Bonds' Place in History Is Secure*." *Sporting News,* May 28, 2007.

Mellinger, Sam, "Segui Talk HGH," *The Kansas City Star,* June 21, 2006.

Mellion, Morris B. "Anabolic Steroids in Athletics." 30 *American Family Physician* 113 (1984).

Nightengale, Bob, "Chemist: MLB Still Has Steroid Issues," *USA Today*, July 26, 2007.

O'Connell, Jack. "Giants-Cubs Delivers Drama." *Hartford Courant*, May 4, 2003.

O'Keefe, Michael. "Conte Sprung, Sees Lying in 'Shadows.'" *New York Daily News*, March 31, 2006.

O'Keefe, Michael and Thompson, Terri, "'Roid Probe Rages on With Bud," *Daily News* (New York), Aug. 9, 2007.

Ostler, Scott. "Barry's Homers Don't Make Him the New Babe." *The San Francisco Chronicle*, July 24, 2003.

"Palmeiro Tests Positive." *Associated Press*, August 1, 2005.

Parker, Rob. "Shame on Aaron for Not Being Supportive of Bonds." *The Detroit News*, April 20, 2007.

Passan, Jeff. "BALCO Case Takes Another Twist." *Yahoo! Sports*. December 28, 2006, www.yahoo.com.

Patrick, Dick, "Sprinter Tells of Descent," *USA Today*, Dec. 3, 2004.

Patrick, Dick and Nightengale, Bob, "Lack of Testing Fuels HGH use," *USA Today*, June 9, 2006.

Petterson, Jean. "Hair Raising." *Orlando Sentinel*, November 18, 2004.

Perlmutter, Gary, and David Lowenthal. "Use of Anabolic Steroids by Athletes," 32 *American Family Physician* 208 (1985).

Pogash, Carol. "Conte Disputes Report That He Gave Steroids to Bonds." *The New York Times*, June 26, 2004.

Pond, Steve, "The Bonds Girl," *Playboy*, November 2007.

Price, S.L. "Dark Times for a Baseball Man." *Sports Illustrated*, June 4, 2007.

Pugmire, Lance. "A Fatal Weekend Fueled by Steroids." *Los Angeles Times*, June 27, 2007.

———. "Jones Admits Using Steroids," *Los Angeles Times*, Oct. 6, 2007.

Quinn, T.J. "Bonds Comes Out Swinging: Sidesteps 'Roids but Not Rage." *New York Daily News*, February 23, 2005.

———. "Bonds Not in Clear: Chemist Hints That Barry Knew," *Daily News* (New York), July 25, 2007.

———. "The HGH Fix," *The Seattle Times*, July 24, 2002.

———. Feds Decide to Balk on Bonds, *Daily News* (New York), July 21, 2006.

———. "Conte Sprints to Bonds' Defense." *New York Daily News*, June 25, 2004.

———. "Failure Leaves a Testy Barry." *New York Daily News*, January 11, 2007.

———. "As Bonds Pursues Aaron, Feds Pursue Case." *New York Daily News*, April 11, 2007.

Rainey, James and Mozingo, Joe. "Reporters in BALCO Scandal Criticized." *Los Angeles Times*, February 16, 2007.

———. "Reporters in BALCO Scandal Criticized," *Los Angeles Times*, Feb. 16, 2007.

Reid, Jason. "Perez Steps Up and Delivers for Dodgers." *Los Angeles Times*, April 17, 2004.

Reilly, Rick. "Paging Dr. Barry." *Sports Illustrated*, December 11, 2006.

———. "The Goods on Barry." *Sports Illustrated*, September 20, 2004.

———. "It's Clear Who's Getting Creamed." *Sports Illustrated*, October 30, 2006.

Roberts, Selena. "Loyalty to Bonds Is Mystifying and Misplaced," *The New York Times*, July 23, 2006, www.select.nytimes.com.

———. "It May Not Be a Pitch That Stops Bonds Short." *The New York Times*, April 4, 2007.

Rosenberg, I.J. "Giants Hoping They Can Build on '97 Success." *The Atlanta Journal and Constitution*, March 8, 1998.

Rosynsky, Paul, "Bonds Hires Lawyers to Fight False Statements," *Contra Costa Times*, Aug. 14, 2007.

Saraceno, Jon, "Canseco Still on a "Truth" Mission,"*USA Today*, July 30, 2007.

Schiller, Diane and Stewart, Richard, "Raid on Steroid "Factory" Nabs 2," *The Houston Chronicle*, Sept. 25, 2007.

Schmaltz, Jim. "The King of Swing." *Muscle & Fitness*, June 2003.

Schmidt, Michael S. "Radomski's Upscale Life Gave No Hint of Drug Dealing." *The New York Times*, April 27, 2007.

Schulman, Henry. "Rockies Pitcher Accuses Bonds." *The San Francisco Chronicle*, February 26, 2004.

Schwarz, Alan. "Scouting Report: The Future Hall of Famer Is Having a Giant Season. Here's Why." *Sports Illustrated for Kids*, September 2001.

Shaikin, Bill, "Bonds Unfazed by Grand Jury," *L.A. Times*, July 22, 2007.

Shea, John. "Bonds Caught in the Act of Being Kind Again." *The San Francisco Chronicle*, October 8, 2001.

Shipgel, Ben. "Breakfast at Julio's." *The New York Times*, March 1, 2006.

Shipley, Amy, "One Mastermind Behind Two Steroids," *The Washington Post*, July 29, 2004.

Shipley, Amy, "This is very Clever Chemistry," *The Washington Post*, Dec. 4, 2004.

Simon, M.D., Harvey B., "Hair Loss: Telling the Bald Truth," *Newsweek*, June 16, 2003.

Singh, R.K., and J. Pooley. "Complete Rupture of the Triceps Brachii Muscle," 36 *British Journal of Sports Medicine* 467 (2002).

Smart, Ian. "Asterisking Barry Bonds." May 4, 2006, www.411mania.com.

Smith, Gary. "What Do We Do Now." *Sports Illustrated*, March 28, 2005.

Suman, Oscar E., et al, "Effect of Exogenous Growth Hormone and Exercise on Lean Mass and Muscle Function in Children with Burns," 94 *Journal of Applied Physiology* 2273-2281 (2003).

Ulner, Mike. "Just Don't Do It, White Warns." *The Toronto Sun*, June 1, 2005.

Verducci, Tom. "Hard Number." *Sports Illustrated*, May 15, 2006.

———. "The Consequences: Now Barry Bonds Could Wind Up Alongside Pete Rose in Baseball Purgatory." *Sports Illustrated*, March 13, 2006.

———. "Is Baseball in the Asterisk Era?" *Sports Illustrated*, March 15, 2004.

———. "Getting Amped: Popping Amphetamines or Other Stimulants Is Part of Many Players' Pregame Routine." *Sports Illustrated*, June 3, 2002.

Walker, Childs, "Effects of HGH a Cloudy Issue, Experts Say: No Lab Evidence Showing Substance Helps Strengthen Athletes," *The Baltimore Sun*, September 11, 2007.

Webby, Sean, "Who is this Man?," *San Jose Mercury News*, Dec. 19, 2004.

Weise, Elizabeth. "LaLanne, Still the Muscle Man." *USA Today*, September 26, 2004.

Werd, Matt, and Leslie Knight. "Healthy Traveler." *AAA Going Places Magazine*, Jul.–Aug. 2004, www.aaagoingplaces.com.

Wharton, David, "Bonds' Attorney Attacks Steroid Allegations," *Los Angeles Times*, April 26, 2004.

Williams, Lance, and Fainaru-Wada, Mark. "What Bonds Told BALCO Grand Jury." *The San Francisco Chronicle*, December 3, 2004.

———. "Bonds' Doctor is Subpoenaed," *San Francisco Chronicle*, April 14, 2006.

———. "ESPN Plays Recording of Trainer Anderson," *San Francisco Chronicle*, July 26, 2007.

———. "Bonds Used Steroids in 2003, Trainer Says on Secret Recording." *San Francisco Chronicle,* October 16, 2004.

———. "BALCO Boss Says He's Victim of 'Personal Vendetta.'" *San Francisco Chronicle,* October 9, 2004.

———. "Bonds' Former Girlfriend Testifies." *San Francisco Chronicle,* March 20, 2005.

———. "Grand Jury End Doesn't Mean Bonds Off Hook." *San Francisco Chronicle,* July 20, 2006.

———. "Baseball Memorabilia Collector Dumping Bonds: He Says Giants Star Drove Down Prices with Forgery Claims." *San Francisco Chronicle,* August 24, 2006.

Wilstein, Steve. "'Andro' Pill OK in Baseball, Not in Other Sports." *Associated Press,* August 21, 1998.

Zillgitt, Jeff. "Bonds, Others Could Do Without Body Armor." *USA Today,* June 24, 2001, www.usatoday.com.

Zinko, Carolyne. "At 60 He Swam to Alcatraz Handcuffed. As He Turns 90, LaLanne Has His Eye on Catalina Channel." *San Francisco Chronicle,* September 24, 2004.

Legal Sources

Bio-Technology General Corp. v. Genentech, Inc. 267 F. 3d 1325 (Fed Cir. 2001).

Braunstein, Glenn. "Anabolic Steroid Use to Enhance Athletes' Performance." 65 *Southern California Law Review* 373 (1991).

Carver v. Bonds 135 Cal. App. 4th 328 (2005).

Collins, Rick. "Changing the Game: The Congressional Response to Sports Doping via the Anabolic Steroid Control Act." 40 *New England Law Review* 753 (2006).

Consumer Justice Center v. Olympian Labs, Inc. 99 Cal. App. 4th 1056 (2002).

In re Grand Jury Subpoenas to Mark Fainaru-Wada and Lance Williams 2006 U.S. Dist. LEXIS 73134 (N. D. Cal. 2006).

In re Grand Jury Subpoenas to Mark Fainaru-Wada and Lance Williams 438 F. Supp. 2d 1111 (N. D. Cal. 2006).

In re Marriage of Bonds 24 Cal. 4th 1 (2000).

In re Marriage of Bonds, 2001 Cal. App. Unpub. LEXIS 87 (2001).

Del Cid, Hector, "Winning at all Costs: Can Major League Baseball's New Drug Policy Deter Kids from Steroids and Maintain the Integrity of the Game," 14 *Sports Lawyers Journal* 169 (2007).

Fortenberry, Paul A.. and Hoffman, Brian E., "Illegal Muscle: A comparative Analysis of Proposed Steroid Legislation and the Policies in Professional Sports' CBAs that Led to the Steroid Controversy," 5 *Virginia Sports & Entertainment Law Journal* 121 (2006) .

Garabaldi, Denise A., "From Grand Slams to Grand Juries: Performance-Enhancing Drug Use in Sports," 40 *New England Law Review* 717 (2006).

Jefferson, Bernard S. (Ret.). "The Hearsay Rule: Determining When Evidence Is Hearsay or Nonhearsay and Determining Its Relevance as One or the Other." 30 *University of West Los Angeles Law Review* 135 (1999).

Latiner, Colin, "Steroids and Drug Enhancements in Sports: The Real Problem and the Real Solution, 3" *Depaul Journal of Sports Law & Contemporary Problems* 192 (2006).

Selig, Allan H. ("Bud"), and Robert D. Manfred Jr., "The Regulation of Nutritional Supplements in Professional Sports." 15 *Stanford Law & Policy Review* 35 (2004). *Sullivan v. Superior Court* 29 Cal. App. 3d 64 (1972).

Osei, David K., "Doping, Juicing, and Executive Bypass Oversight: A Case Study of Major League Baseball's Steroid Scandal, 4" *Virginia Sports & Entertainment Law Journal* 155 (2004).

United States of America v. Comprehensive Drug Testing, Inc. 473 F.3d 915 (9th Cir. 2006).

United States Anti-Doping Agency v. Floyd Landis, American Arbitration Association No. 30 190 00847 06, September 20, 2007.

United States of America v. Conte 2004 U.S. Dist. LEXIS 25896 (2004).

United States of America v. Conte, USDC Case No CR 04-0044 SI (N. D. Cal.) (Order Re: Motions to Dismiss, Motions to Quash and Discovery Motions).

United States of America v. Varsalona 710 F. 2d 418 (8th Cir. 1983).

Websites

www.aphroditejones.com
www.ballparks.com
www.baseball-almanac.com
www.baseballlibrary.com
www.baseballprospectus.com
www.baseball-reference.com
www.baseball-statistics.com
www.bodybuildingsecrets.com
www.boombats.com
www.creatinemonohydrate.net
www.darinsteen.com
www.discoveracneinfo.com
www.espn.go.com
www.giftofstrength.com
www.healthyweightforum.org
www.hitrunscore.com
www.irs.gov
www.kidshealth.org
www.mayoclinic.com
www.medscape.com
www.midwestchristianbodybuilding.com
www.nabba.com
www.nba.com
www.nida.nih.gov
www.outside.away.com

www.sandowmuseum.com
www.thedeadballera.com
www.thesmokinggun.com
www.usatoday.com
www.webmd.ccm

Index

Rodriguez, Ivan, 50
Romanowski, Bill, 158, 170
*Ron Kittle's Tales from the White
    Sox Dugout* (Kittle), 17, 18,
    19
Rookie of the Year, 34
Rose, Pete, v, 185
Ross, Mark, 9
Ruth, Babe, x, xi, 17, 23, 38, 46, 63,
    64, 65, 80, 81, 96, 99, 100,
    109, 113, 114, 126, 129, 148,
    151, 161, 187, 189
    improvements in game, ix–x
Ruth, George Herman. *See* Ruth,
    Babe
Ryan, Nolan, 99

S
Salmons, Tim, 147
Sam Bat, 138, 139, 140
Sample, Billy, 137
San Francisco Chronicle, 14, 59
San Francisco Giants, 6, 11–12, 14,
    19, 27, 29, 131, 146
    training camp, 14
Santangelo, F.P., 8
Santiago, Benito, 67, 70, 165
Schilling, Curt, 20, 56, 176
Schmidt, Mike, viii, 21, 22, 23, 24,
    121, 122, 132, 133, 136, 138,
    139, 141, 142
Schwarzenegger, Arnold, 42, 108
Scott, Paul, 20

Scottsdale, Arizona, 14
Seattle Mariners, 107
Sekera, Michael, 69
17-alkylated compounds, 48
sexual dysfunction, 104–107
Sharmon, Bill, 115, 116
Sheffield, Gary, 67, 81, 100,
    101
Shoe size, 109–110
Siciliano, Angelo. *See* Atlas,
    Charles
Sills, David, 48–49
Silva, Mark, 101, 102
Simon, Harvey, Dr., 108
Simon, Michael, 7, 8
Sinin, Lee, 64
Snider, Duke, 187
somatotropin, 44
Sosa, Sammy, 7, 18, 20, 53, 54, 56,
    60, 63, 69, 95, 113, 117, 143,
    144, 172
Spahn, Warren, 143, 144
Speaker, Tris, 128
Splendid Splinter
    See Williams, Ted
Sports Illustrated, xi, 14, 21
St. Louis Cardinals, 36, 49
stanozolol. *See* Winstrol
Stargell, Willie, 10
Steen, Darin, 94, 95, 96, 99
Steinfeldt, Harry, 115
Steroid Bible, The (Gallaway),
    173–174